# doing
# justice
# together

MICHAEL ADAM BECK
STEPHANIE MOORE HAND

# doing
# justice
# together

*Fresh Expressions Pathways
for Healing in Your Church*

Abingdon Press™
*Nashville*

DOING JUSTICE TOGETHER
*Copyright © 2024 by Abingdon Press*

ISBN: 9781791032791

Library of Congress Control Number has been requested.

Scripture quotations marked CEB are from the Common English Bible. Copyright © 2011 by the Com-mon English Bible. All rights reserved. Used by permission. www.CommonEnglishBible.com.

Scripture quotations unless otherwise noted are taken from the New Revised Standard Version Updated Edition. Copyright © 2021 National Council of Churches of Christ in the United States of America. Used by permission. All rights reserved worldwide.

Scripture quotations marked (NIV) are taken from the Holy Bible, New International Version®, NIV®. Copyright © 1973, 1978, 1984, 2011 by Biblica, Inc.™ Used by permission of Zondervan. All rights reserved worldwide. www.zondervan.com The "NIV" and "New International Version" are trademarks registered in the United States Patent and Trademark Office by Biblica, Inc.™

Scripture quotations noted KJV are from The Authorized (King James) Version. Rights in the Authorized Version in the United Kingdom are vested in the Crown. Reproduced by permission of the Crown's pat-entee, Cambridge University Press.

MANUFACTURED IN THE UNITED STATES OF AMERICA

# Contents

# Acknowledgments

We would like to acknowledge the circle of companions who accompanied us in *Doing Justice Together*.

Sincere thanks to Dr. Liz Piatt of Kent State University for her helpful feedback with the manuscript. Deep gratitude to Rev. Dr. Candace Lewis, President-Dean of Gammon Theological Seminary for being an insightful conversation partner over the years. Also, shot out to Rev. Dr. Elizabeth Ríos Founder & President at Passion2Plant Network, for giving us space to test run these ideas with practitioners.

We are deeply indebted to each brave person who contributed their voice and story to this work, Reverend Mother Geraldine McCellan, Rev. Kris Sledge, Rev. Tiffany McCall, Lona R Seymour, Rev. Woo Kang, Rev. Sadell Bradley, Jordan Shaw, Jaidymar Smith, Rev. Raimon Jackson, Dr, Elizabeth Ríos, Tracy Rose, and Abedabun "she who sees in the distance" (her Ojibwe name), also endearingly known to many as the Reverend Dawn Houser.

Stephanie would like to extend heartfelt gratitude to those through your lived experiences with me, helped me to bring this book to life. Your unwavering support and belief in equity and justice for all inspire me. My mother, Alva Lee Scott Moore, grandmother, Mollie Scott Burnett, Olive Mae Godette, and great-grandmother, Annie Gaskill Wilder, exemplified for me justice, mercy, and humility.

I am grateful for my high school Coach, Edith Styron, who stood in the gap for me during a racial attack. Life Long high school friends Kris Mckay, Carmetha Williams, Audra Tillery, and church friends Karen Perry, Robin Berkey, and Suzie Stephenson, your presence and honest conversations are invaluable.

The Metro District of the UMC community's commitment to following God's lead for discipleship is genuinely inspiring.

Sisters in Christ and prayer partners, Rev. Sharon Washington, Rev. Pamela Blackstock, and Rev. Dr. Veronica Palmer, Tonja Sholtz, and Tonya Little, reveal the transformative power of prayer. Bishops Latrelle Easterling, Cynthia Moore-Koikoi, Sharma Lewis, and Tracie Malone, your encouragement and leadership are exemplary. Dr. Peter Story, thank you for your wisdom, which has been invaluable.

Thank you, Rev Mother Geraldine McClellan, a pioneer in the church who continues to mentor emerging Black pastors. Reminding me never to quit when it gets ugly and nasty because this is noble work in which God is still in control.

Thank you, Bishop Ken Carter, for your allyship and willingness to stand even when people throw rocks to harm.

To my husband, Walter "Chip" Hand Jr., and our young adults, PK's Ashlee, and Walter III, your unwavering support means everything.

Lastly, I thank God for inspiring Dr. Michael Beck's vision of collaboration with me to make a difference in the Kingdom of God.

Michael would like to thank the Florida congregations who lived through this journey together. Especially the WildOnes of Wildwood who stayed the course through many dangers, toils, and snares. To the people of Royal, your "pink socked preacher" is still carrying the flame. "The roof, the roof, the roof, is on fire, we don't need no water…" Your anointing of oil and laying on of hands was my most meaningful ordination, a symbol of your trust and love. To God's Glory Ministries for literally moving "God's Glory" into the building. Pastor Albert Taylor and first lady Cynthia Taylor, Eric Wilkins, and Dwayne Butler, you are appreciated.

To the St Markans in Ocala who are doing the work today. To the sister, co-laborer, Pastor and Prophet, Betti Jefferson, an eternal friend. To the Right Reverend Octavius Smith (AKA Bishop Smith) a lifelong traveling companion.

To Rev. Dr. Sharon Austin for leading Florida in this work and showing me how to march beside her in the footsteps of Dr. King. To Rev. Dr. David Allen, our fearless district superintendent, dean, professor, and friend. And finally, to the Bishop's Task Force on Anti-Racism in the Florida UMC, thanks for living out together what this book calls for.

To the students of the Fresh Expressions House of Studies at United Theological Seminary. You have each been a gift to me. We created this book together through our many prayerful conversations. I have learned more than I ever taught.

Lastly and most importantly I would like to thank my wife, co-pastor, and best friend, Jill Beck who has led, supported, and walked every step of this journey alongside me.

# Togetheversity

There goes momma Mary,
Bearing down, heaving away.
Flashback to a barn cave,
Smelled like animal feces.
Now, odorous with sweaty fasting bodies,
Huddled together in that room.
Then, laid her newborn in a feeding trough.
Now, birthing a new body.
She's been fervent,
Since the water broke from his pierced side,
On a hill called the skull.
Woosh, a gust of wind,
From a giant dove,
That can wrap the world in love with her wingspan.
Kindles a flame again,
That once blazed in the thornbush,
And showed as a shekinah fire pillar,
Lighting up the wilderness night,
By day, a smoke tower to the sky.
Now those many colored bodies,
Sweat drenched in the smell of fasting,
Were oil and kindling for the flame.
Together they sang one story,
With every tongue under heaven.
Mary, eyes ablaze, cracks a smile.
She did it again.
Her baby boy lives on.
In an uncountable sea of bodies like cells.
Now joined together as his one body.
Eternal and indestructible.
Together.
Diversity.
Togetheversity.

~*Michael Adam Beck*

# Opening Vision
## All the Families of the Earth

*". . . all the families of the earth will be blessed because of you."*
*(Genesis 12:3)*

Racism is anti-Christian.

It is not a secondary or social issue—it is a sin issue. Racism is antithetical to the gospel of Jesus Christ. It is a sin that harms everyone involved at some level.

Jesus was the fulfillment of an ancient promise that stretched back all the way to the obscure wandering family of Abraham and Sarah. This family, called out from the civilization they knew to go on a journey toward a promised land, would become the ancestral parents of a people in whom all the tribes would be blessed (Genesis 12:1-3). A vision of all the diverse tribes of humanity living in a blessed communion has been called the "Abrahamic Promise."

The church is to be a sign, instrument, and foretaste of this diverse but unified reality, one aspect of which includes interracial unity and multi-ethnic flourishing.[1] So, we must ask, why does the church look even more segregated than society all around her and how did she get that way? In this book we move beyond analysis of the current reality to explore what role the church can play in seeing all the families of the earth living in blessed communion. How can the church help heal the world?

---

1. Newbigin, Lesslie. *Foolishness to the Greeks: The Gospel and Western Culture* (Grand Rapids, MI: Wm. B. Eerdmans Publishing Co., 1986), 98.

# Togetheversity

To describe all the families of the earth living in blessed communion, we need a new word.

The apostle Paul was adept at creating new words to describe kingdom mysteries. In a letter to Timothy, attempting to help his protégé be faithful and fruitful during a challenging time, he wrote:

"All Scripture is *God-breathed* and is useful for teaching, rebuking, correcting and training in righteousness . . ." (2 Timothy 3:16 NIV, emphasis ours).

He creates a new word, only used once in the New Testament, and with no apparent equivalent use in any literature preceding Paul. The word is θεόπνευστος (*theopneustos*), which many versions of the Bible translate as *God-breathed* or *inspired by God*. It is the combination of two words, *theos* – "God" and *pneustos* – "breathed." In instructing Timothy about the nature, importance, authority, of scripture for study, correction, and reproof within the community, there was not a word that would suffice. So, as theologians who try to use finite and limited words to describe God-sized mysteries often do, Paul created a new one.

We believe the same is true when we describe the miraculous and universal nature of how God has fulfilled the Abrahamic Promise through Jesus Christ. In the first Pentecost, God literally creates a new humanity (Acts 2).

When Pentecost Day arrived, they were all together in one place. Suddenly a sound from heaven like the howling of a fierce wind filled the entire house where they were sitting. They saw what seemed to be individual flames of fire alighting on each one of them. They were all filled with the Holy Spirit and began to speak in other languages as the Spirit enabled them to speak.

There were pious Jews from every nation under heaven living in Jerusalem. When they heard this sound, a crowd gathered. They were mystified because everyone heard them speaking in their native languages. They were surprised and amazed, saying, "Look, aren't all the people who are speaking Galileans, every one of them? How then can each of us hear them speaking in our native language? Parthians, Medes, and Elamites; as well as residents of Mesopotamia, Judea, and Cappadocia, Pontus and Asia, Phrygia and Pamphylia, Egypt and the regions of Libya bordering Cyrene; and visitors from Rome (both Jews and converts to Judaism), Cretans and Arabs—we hear them declaring the mighty works of God in our own languages!" They were all surprised and bewildered. Some asked each other, "What does this mean?" (Acts 2:1-12 CEB)

What does this mean indeed? The outpouring of the Spirit at Pentecost was one of the most transformative moments in human history. Afterward, when Peter, empowered by the Spirit, begins to preach, he points to its significance as being fulfilled by the prophet Joel . . .

This is what was spoken through the prophet Joel:

> "In the last days it will be, God declares,
>    that I will pour out my Spirit upon all flesh,
>       and your sons and your daughters shall prophesy,
>    and your young men shall see visions,
>       and your old men shall dream dreams.
> Even upon my slaves, both men and women,
>    in those days I will pour out my Spirit,
>       and they shall prophesy.
> And I will show portents in the heaven above
>    and signs on the earth below,
>       blood, and fire, and smoky mist.
> The sun shall be turned to darkness
>    and the moon to blood,
>       before the coming of the Lord's great and glorious day.
> Then everyone who calls on the name of the Lord
>    shall be saved."
>                    (Acts 2:16-21 CEB)

God is pouring out the Spirit "upon all flesh." Not just a select few anointed ones, but everybody.

What we see in that first outpouring of the Spirit is *togetherness*. The disciples are united in prayer, *together* in one place. We also see *diversity*. Representatives from every tribe and tongue under heaven together in one place.

*Togetheversity*. There is unity, oneness, *koinonia*. There is also diversity, distinctness, including every ethnos. A plurality of people and languages, hearing each other, singing the same story.

In the Book of Revelation, we get to peer through the curtain into the new creation just behind the veil. In that coming-soon future we see,

> After this I looked, and there was a great multitude that no one could count, from every nation, from all tribes and peoples and languages, standing before the throne and before the Lamb, robed in white, with palm branches in their hands. They cried out in a loud voice, saying,
>
> "Salvation belongs to our God who is seated on the throne and to the Lamb!"
>
> (Revelation 7:9)

In that vision, we see Jesus's earthly prayer finally fully answered, "Thy kingdom come, Thy will be done in earth, as it is in heaven" (Matthew 6:10 KJV). We see the final fulfillment of the Abrahamic Promise and the conclusion of the outpouring of the Spirit at Pentecost. There is not a word in any language that adequately describes this illusive reality.

Most of us have personal experience with how certain words immediately shut down conversations that could lead to healing. Thus, in the line of our spiritual matriarchs and patriarchs we are suggesting a new one: "togetheversity."

# Racialization

Racialization refers to the larger reality of harmful stereotypes, ideas, policies, and structures, that divides human beings made in the image of God into race categories. We believe God's ultimate desire for this sin-warped way to structure the world is *healing*. "Christ . . . gave us the ministry of reconciliation" (2 Corinthians 5:18) and one aspect of reconciliation is healing among all the tribes and peoples of the earth.

In this book, we offer a pathway for the healing of racialization. We believe churches can and must be a key instrument in this work.

We acknowledge right up front that in the words of historian and author Ibram Kendi, "Race is a genetic mirage."[2] Genetically speaking, all human beings, regardless of skin pigmentation are 99.9 the same. As Genesis 1:27 informs us, all human beings are created in the image of God. We have a shared humanity that flows from the diversity of our creator God.

However, while race is *not real*, it is an illusion, racism and racialization *are very much real*. And Christianity has played an essential function in perpetuating racism in the United States.[3] The social construct of race came into being in the sixteenth and seventeenth centuries, largely to justify the capture, abuse, and sale of black and brown bodies, and was intended to create a hierarchy. As the authors of *The 1619 Project* document in detail, the USA is a nation built upon the back of the Atlantic Slave Trade. Every structural system of US society, political, economic, social, and religious has its roots in the soils of slavery. That system of racialization continues to place people of color at the bottom of the hierarchy to this day. Isabel Wilkerson defines this structure as a caste system.[4]

Oneya Okuwobi highlights the fact that the racial reconciliation and multiethnic church movements have failed.[5] The Barna 2021 study, *Beyond Diversity, reported that fewer than half of white Christians who attend multiethnic congregations agree that the US has historically been oppressive to people of color;*[6] the majority of white Christians believe individuals of color are treated similarly to white people;[7] and yet the report discovered that black Christians in multiethnic churches are more likely to experience racial prejudice, have difficulty building relationships, and are largely

2. Kendi, Ibram X. How to be an Antiracist (New York: One World), 53.

3. Emerson, Michael O., and Christian Smith. *Divided by Faith: Evangelical Religion and the Problem of Race in America* (Oxford, NY: Oxford University Press, 2000), 14.

4. Wilkerson, Isabel. *Caste: The Origins of Our Discontents* (First edition. New York: Random House, 2020), 21.

5. Okuwobi, Oneya. "Moving Forward on Race" in Smith, L. Rowland, Michael Adam Beck, Alan Hirsch, Leonard Sweet, Brian Sanders, Gregory Coles, Jay Y. Kim, et al. *Red Skies: 10 Essential Conversations Exploring Our Future as the Church (Cody, WY: 100 Movements Publishing, 2022).*

6. Barna Group, *Beyond Diversity* (Ventura, CA: Barna Group, 2021), 34.

7. Ibid., 46.

denied leadership positions.[8] Robert Jones's *White Too Long* explores the historical relationship between the church and white supremacy in depth.[9]

We believe that racial reconciliation, as it has been understood thus far, and multiethnic congregations are not enough. Local churches must organize to engage in the work of antiracism—the policy or practice of opposing racism and promoting racial equality. We need to challenge and reorganize the systems that perpetuate inequity and the continued harm and oppression of persons of color.

To stop short of this is in fact anti-Christian.

## A Pathway for Healing Racialization

In the face of the realities of racialization, to form beloved communities of togetheversity that heal, the people of God must "do justice together."

We draw this phrase from the prophet Micah, who was crying out against the injustices of his own day . . .

> He has told you, O mortal, what is good,
>     and what does the Lord require of you
> but to *do justice* and to love kindness
> and to walk humbly with your God?
>                     (Micah 6:8, italics ours)

To "do justice" is not a passive posture. It requires prayerful action. The death-dealing features of racialization will not simply disappear or vanish if we ignore them long enough. It requires the people of God to live the kind of life that Micah envisions—and to do so in community, together.

In this book we offer a pathway for the healing of racialization. This journey can be understood as a series of circles, each of which may be widening simultaneously at different paces. *Doing Justice Together occurs in the*

---

8. Ibid., 26.

9. Jones, Robert P. *White Too Long: The Legacy of White Supremacy in American Christianity* (New York: Simon & Schuster, 2020).

*mandorla, the sacred space where the circles overlap. The pathway for healing racialization involves:*

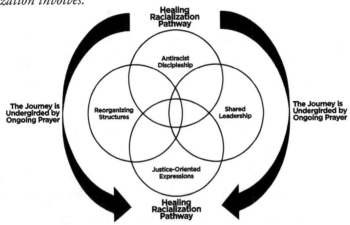

1. Antiracist Discipleship: A prayerful process of engagement with biblical and historical sources that helps congregations go on a journey of *metanoia* (a transformation of heart and mind, repentance).

2. Shared Leadership: A prayerful process of sharing power, in which persons of color inhabit equal positions of leadership throughout the congregation/organization/society (Acts 6:1-7).

3. Justice-Oriented Expressions: A prayerful journey of cultivating new Christian communities throughout a parish or region, which have an internal motivation to include diversity (Luke 10:1-9).

4. Reorganizing Structures: A prayerful, strategic, and cooperative effort of congregations to join other activists, groups, organizations, and faith communities to challenge identified features of structural racism in local, regional, and national systems (Micah 6:8).

# Expanding Circles

We have chosen "expanding circles" as our primary image based on the insights of African theologian Mercy Amba Oduyoye who notes that a circle expands forever,

It turns outward to interact with the outside
And inward for self critique[10]

Each circle on this pathway is an ever-expanding sphere of inclusion, not a stage or phase to complete. These circles ripple forth into the new creation, encapsulating both the personal and communal dimensions of sanctifying grace.

It's important to note that many Christians have struggled against slavery, segregation, and Jane and Jim Crow. Our model builds upon that legacy but takes it further, providing a practical theological framework that leads to social change both in the church and society at large. We must do this to authentically pray with Jesus, "Thy kingdom come, Thy will be done in earth, as it is in heaven" (Matthew 6:10 KJV).

We want to begin by providing the "why" for this book and articulating our hope for what it might contribute to the healing of our world.

The two of us are not removed from the subject matter. While each of us has doctoral degrees, we are not ivory tower scholars formulating these ideas completely removed from frontline action. We are practitioners of ministry, involved in the day-to-day shepherding of souls toward God amid the daily struggles of life. In that vocation, we are also each involved in the work of healing racialization. Stephanie as a Director working at a regional level across Western North Carolina, and Michael both as a Director working at a national level and among a local network of congregations in Florida.

We also each bring our own life experiences, history, and blind spots to this conversation. Our blind spots include a lack of personal knowledge in the experience of racism among Latin, Asian, Indigenous, and Middle Eastern persons. We cannot speak of those realities from a firsthand perspective. We can only speak from the humble and limited perspective of our own understanding and interactions. As a hetero black female, and

---

10.    Mercy Amba Oduyoye, "The Story of a Circle" (Circle of Concerned African Women Theologians) *The Ecumenical Review*, vol. 53, no. 1 (Jan. 2001): 97.

a hetero white male, we have each experienced the harm of racism and participated in it in different ways.

We also realize our limitations as citizens born and raised in the USA. While our own vision is limited, the hope of the Abrahamic Promise includes all people everywhere.

We have invited friends to share stories of healing racialization in their own lives in an attempt to bring other perspectives to this conversation. They are black, brown, native. They are straight and queer. And we celebrate their courage to share their stories in these pages and in the audio and video companion versions that can be found at the Fresh Expressions channel at Amplifymedia.com.[11] We hope what we offer has larger applications.

## "Much More to Be Done"

*Reverend Mother Geraldine McClellan*
*First Ordained African American Female Elder in the Florida Conference of the*
*United Methodist Church 1980 Deacon, 1982 Elder in Full Connection*

There is so much that could be said—but there's not enough time. I am a PK—a preacher's kid of the Central Jurisdiction. My grandfather, my father, his two brothers, and other relatives were preachers. At that time, the Central Jurisdiction had no real meaning to us; we were children. It wasn't until we were teenagers involved in the MYF—Methodist Youth fellowship—that we heard the stories of the separation and how divisive it became.

I could say much more—but I thank God for the Central Jurisdiction—I don't want to speak for others, but The Central Jurisdiction provided us training ground—we were shaped and molded into leaders by being allowed to serve beside strong leaders both lay and clergy—I think about Mrs. Gertrude Stiles who served as conference youth director—pastors to many to name who encouraged us to use our gifts and

---

11.    https://my.amplifymedia.com/freshexpressions/home

talents. The central jurisdiction prepared us for the change that was to come eventually.

And it came—April 23, 1968, the wind of change eliminated the central jurisdiction by actions of the General Conference with the merger of the Methodist and Evangelical United Brethren churches into the United Methodist Church. My Uncle, my father's brother, the Rev. JBF Williams, was appointed as the first black DS—he passed in 1971, and Rev. Ernest Newman replaced him. Rev. Newman was appointed to the first cross-cultural appointment in the Florida Conference—Plantation UMC. He was one of two episcopal candidates from the Florida Conference in 1984, along with Rev. J. Lloyd Knox were both elected. The phone would not stop ringing—tears of joy flooded our souls.

Both of these bishops, along with Rev. Aaron D. Hall. Rev. William Ferguson, Rev. E.J. Shephard, and Rev. A. L. Pearce were pastors who walked beside me on my journey into ministry. The encouragement when I felt like giving up—I can Hear them even now saying to me you've come too far to turn back now. My journey would not have been possible had it not been for the Central Jurisdiction that nurtured me.

My experience of being called to ministry began as a child. A great cloud of witnesses surrounded me. My grandfather, father, uncles, and other family members served as Pastors in the Central Jurisdiction of the Methodist Church. I was always overwhelmed by the commitment and compassion of my parents as they ministered to the total person, regardless of race. I watched their giving spirit in the midst of segregation, providing for the least of these.

It was then, at the young age of about nine years old, that I felt a tugging within my heart. It was in 1967 when I acknowledged my call to ministry; leaders told me that God did call women to preach and referred to 1 Corinthians 14:34-35 "Women should be silent in the churches. They are not permitted to speak but should be subordinate, as the law also says. If there is anything they desire to know, let them ask their husbands at home. For it is shameful for a woman to speak in church."

The hardest part about being a woman in ministry is setting boundaries and finding a way to be effective without being burned out as we seek to find the balance between the responsibilities of spouse, mother, and pastor and trying to build in time for self-care and personal reflection.

The biggest surprise about filling this role – is to expect surprises. You can't prepare for them, but you can determine how you respond to them. And that includes the good ones and the bad ones.

From the beginning of my journey into ordained ministry in the Florida Annual Conference, I experienced the prejudice, the bias of those on the Board of Ordained Ministry. They were not initially interested in the articulation of my call or theology or sermon preparation; they were more interested in where I came from and my lifestyle. The line of questioning told me, "You Don't Fit." I went before the Florida UM Board of Ordinary Ministry five times. Each time someone said there was no place for a Black Female Clergy, they told me I should quit and never come back. As children, my siblings and our parents taught us never to give up or in. If you believe in your heart that you are moving in God's will, let nothing stand in the way of you following God's lead—and I did not. Five times I was rejected by the Florida Conference Board of Ordained Ministry but with a tenacious spirit kept going back, and the sixth time I made it through. The journey hasn't been easy, but with God, it has been worth it.

The doors are open to receive women pastors, but the opportunity for service is limited. The glass ceiling in the annual conference has a small crack in it, but it's not visible. Women are reduced to two-point charges, small congregations, dying, and conflicting settings without support. Those who are in the larger congregations or in leadership positions find little time, if any, to mentor those who could one day take their places.

When I entered the ministry, there were no clergy support groups. I tried reaching out but was not invited to the inner tables of leaders. It was and is a lonely journey when there is no one to connect with and willing to walk alongside you. I strongly encourage clergy to connect with a clergy support group as soon as possible or start with those who have journeyed with them.

The current climate for women pastors in the Florida Conference is better than it has been in the past, but there is still much more to be done in the church to become more inclusive of using women's gifts. Both female and male clergy tend to be used in specific areas based on their likability and willingness to conform to the status quo. Those with differing views and opinions tend to be left out.

# CHAPTER 1

# A Pathway for Healing Racialization

*They will rebuild ancient ruins on your account;*
*the foundations of generations past you will restore.*
*You will be called Mender of Broken Walls,*
*Restorer of Livable Streets.*
*(Isaiah 58:12 CEB)*

In this book, we offer a practical framework to help congregations along the journey of healing racialization. This journey takes learnings from the successes and failures of key movements toward racial equality, and suggests some additional steps that integrate those previous movements.

We suggest the language of a pathway as an image of ever-widening circles, because we believe healing racialization is just that, it is a journey that will not be complete in this life. Just as sin seems to be a reality that clings to this very good creation, so is racism, its offspring. Ultimately, just as we are entirely dependent on the return of Jesus for the unleashing of a renewed cosmos, we are equally so regarding the pervasive realities of racialization.

However, here we must heed the warning of Dr Keri Day, professor of constructive theology and African American religion, regarding how we situate human agency in relation to divine agency. If the Messiah alone is the singular agent who brings about the "Messianic Age," the final point of universal peace and justice, we "may not allow enough room for humans to work creatively toward peace and justice."[1]

We must hold this understanding of Jesus as the primary agent who inaugurates this messianic reign, in tension with our calling to act prayerfully as "peacemakers" (Matthew 5:9 NRSVUE) who "do justice" in the meantime (Micah 6:8).

In Isaiah 58, God speaking through the prophet is announcing the people's rebellion and calling out their sins. The people seem to be doing all the right things, observing their religious rituals, and even fasting. Yet God seems to ask, "you call this a fast?" (Isaiah 58:4-5 NRSVUE). All their religious practices seem to actually be an affront to God. Their prayers are useless, their worship services are aggravating, and their fasts are hollow. God then speaks,

> Isn't this the fast I choose:
>> releasing wicked restraints, untying the ropes of a yoke,
>> setting free the mistreated,
>> and breaking every yoke?
> Isn't it sharing your bread with the hungry
>> and bringing the homeless poor into your house,
>> covering the naked when you see them,
>> and not hiding from your own family?
> Then your light will break out like the dawn,
>> and you will be healed quickly.
> Your own righteousness will walk before you,
>> and the Lord's glory will be your rear guard.
> Then you will call, and the Lord will answer;
>> you will cry for help, and God will say, "I'm here."
> If you remove the yoke from among you,
>> the finger-pointing, the wicked speech;
>> if you open your heart to the hungry,
>> and provide abundantly for those who are afflicted,

---

1. Day, Keri *Religious Resistance to Neoliberalism: Womanist and Black Feminist Perspectives* (Houndmills, Basingstoke, Hampshire, UK: Palgrave Macmillan, 2015), 28.

> your light will shine in the darkness,
>> and your gloom will be like the noon.
> The Lord will guide you continually
>> and provide for you, even in parched places.
> He will rescue your bones.
> You will be like a watered garden,
>> like a spring of water that won't run dry.
>> (Isaiah 58: 6-11 CEB)

This is a call to integrate prayer and practice, words and action, faith and works. Yet the most beautiful section of this passage follows next,

> Your ancient ruins shall be rebuilt;
>> you shall raise up the foundations of many generations;
>> *you shall be called the repairer of the breach,*
>> the restorer of streets to live in.
>> (Isaiah 58:12 NRSVUE, italics ours)

Here is a vision for the future that fulfills the ancient promises. It's about renewal and rebuilding something that was broken down and decaying. Yet this restoration will be the "foundation" for many future generations. Then comes our favorite line, you will become, "repairers of the breach" רָדַג (*gādar* "repairer") פֶרֶץ (*pereṣ* "breach"). A breach can be both a gap in a wall or barrier, and an act of breaking or failing to observe an agreement, or code of conduct. Something that was once a structure of integrity is now fragmented. A relationship that was once whole is now broken.

In this scenario, God is calling upon his people to be "repairers" who seal and reinforce the broken structure. Those who reconcile the relationships and bandage the wounds. Where there is harm, they bring healing.

We think this language is perfect when it comes to healing racialization. There has been a "breach" in the integrity of our social system. There has been fragmentation in our shared humanity. Racism is a wound that hurts us all, but it is particularly harmful to persons of color. In the

**3**

hierarchy that racialization creates and sustains, white people find themselves at the top of a pyramid of oppression. This is not a good place for whites to be, for as James Cone reminds us, the God we encounter in Jesus is a God of the oppressed, and theology must "arise out of an oppressed community as they seek to understand their place in the history of salvation."[2] God is against the oppressor.

Perhaps white people did not intentionally put themselves here, but they are here, nevertheless. The pyramid seems invisible in some ways to those at the top but is blatantly obvious to those at the bottom. We are not looking each other in the eyes. Racialization creates a scenario in which some people are looking down from a position of privilege and power.

This "breach" cannot be healed by simply more or better religious practice, more prayer, more worship, more fasting. As formative and life-giving as those practices may be, they must lead us to action that reflects the "the kind of fasting" God requires (Isaiah 58:6 NIV).

To repair something, we have to act. We have to physically reconstruct the broken places in the structure. We have to actively seek to right the relational wrongs, to make amends for the harm we have caused. We have to dismantle the invisible pyramid that we find ourselves inhabiting from different unequal vantage points. This action will require changing structures and policies that maintain the status quo of racialization. And it will require us to do so in community, as fruitful branches connected to the vine (John 15).

We cannot "bring the kingdom," but we can be instruments of it. We cannot force the new creation into existence by our own actions, but we can become the ingredients of it. In that way, we can bear fruit that will last.

So, we suggest a framework that can be understood as a journey—a series of movements that enable us to "do justice together." The journey is a rhythm of ongoing prayerful action. We don't have to break those

---

2. Cone, James H., God of the Oppressed. Rev. ed. (Maryknoll, NY: Orbis Books, 1997), 6.

two things apart, prayer and action. Instead, we integrate prayer with the movements and actions throughout the journey.

This pathway for healing racialization involves four ever-widening circles of inclusion:

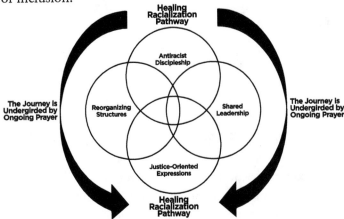

Note the overall circular and cyclical nature of the framework. It is an ongoing movement through the expanding dimensions: personal, communal, societal, and structural. The directional arrows are intentionally moving both ways. This journey may start with a commitment to personal discipleship that addresses racist thinking and actions, which moves to reorganizing oppressive structures at a societal level. Yet it could also begin with a group of people working together to reorganize structures that maintain inequality, who then decide to start a new expression together, or commit to deepen spiritual maturity through mutually agreed upon practices.

Each circle may be expanding at different rates and at different times. Some might not be expanding at all, even atrophying. The journey includes seeking to expand each dimension so that justice encompasses more and more of every facet of life and society.

Here we will briefly describe the four movements. The coming chapters explore each more deeply.

1. Discipleship: Sanctification as Antiracism: A prayerful process of engagement with biblical and historical sources that

helps people and congregations go on a journey of metanoia (a transformation of heart and mind, or repentance). This is a journey of unlearning racist ideas, actions, and policies, to replace them with biblical, antiracist ideas, actions, and policies (Galatians 3:28). This equates to ongoing sanctification in the lifelong journey of grace.

2.  Shared Leadership: A prayerful process of sharing power, in which persons of color inhabit equal positions of leadership throughout the congregation/organization (Acts 6). This moves beyond the current "multicultural church movement," which often still operates under the assumptions of white supremacy. It seeks to distribute power equally, including persons of color as equals in decision-making. It also seeks equitable compensation for everyone involved and guards against the racial disparities we noted earlier. Within the shared leadership movement is also a commitment to abolish "tokenism," which refers to the practice of making only a perfunctory or symbolic effort to recruit a small number of people from underrepresented groups in order to give the appearance of racial equality, which is in reality misleading.

3.  Justice-Oriented Expressions: A prayerful journey of cultivating new beloved communities throughout a parish or region, which have an internal motivation to include diversity (Luke 10:1-10). These communities make one aspect of their life a commitment to social justice. These emerging communities live in a blended ecology with inherited congregations. This movement combines social justice and contextual church planting. We refer to it as justice-oriented church planting, but at the most basic level, it is an effort to join God's diversity, which is often absent in seemingly segregated congregations. This focuses discipleship toward outreaching love, rather than on simply fulfilling religious responsibilities. This sort of discipleship grows into "loosing the bonds of injustice" . . . "freeing the oppressed" . . . "breaking yokes" . . . "sharing bread with the hungry" . . . "sheltering the homeless" . . . "clothing the naked" (see Isaiah 58:6-7). It helps us strengthen relationships through loving and serving our community.

4. Reorganizing Structures: A prayerful, strategic, and cooperative effort of congregations to join other activists, groups, organizations, and faith communities to challenge identified features of structural racism in local, regional, and national systems as we "do justice" together (see Micah 6:8). This includes reorganizing societal systems by seeking to change laws and policies that perpetuate inequality. It enables us to join grassroots efforts that can aim at legislation, but simultaneously build relationships with others engaged in the struggle. We will suggest that Mahatma Gandhi's approach to accomplishing societal reorganization needs to be revisited. Satyagraha, "soul force" or "love force" or "truth force," was Gandhi's way of nonviolent resistance, peaceful protest, and mass fasts. His approach was taken up by Dr. King and others in the Civil Rights Movement.

Together, these ever-widening circles offer a wholistic way for congregations to approach healing the racialization that exists at every level of society.

# The Next Step

The *Doing Justice* pathway encourages us to begin with a small group of people. This team will explore a deeper discipleship that forces us to confront our own isms, learn how to share power, cultivate justice-oriented communities, and then affect the oppressive structures of a racialized society. Concluding each chapter, "The Next Step" sections are designed to work through together as a team. After each chapter is a story from one of our brave friends who boldly shares their journey of pain, trauma, and healing. Following the stories are a few questions for your team to talk through together. In addition to the written stories in this book, a series of companion audio-video stories are provided at the Fresh Expressions channel on Amplify Media.[3] We encourage your team to watch or listen together, share them in worship, and reflect upon them together.

---

3.  https://my.amplifymedia.com/freshexpressions/home

- As you begin to explore the pathway, we want to invite you to prayerfully consider who you might need to include. This is not a journey to be taken alone. The team will be less effective if it includes only insiders, or long-time members of your congregation. On your team, it might be helpful if you think of these relational circles:

- Core: a group of core committed disciples who are stakeholders in the congregation.

- Fringe: consider people who are loosely connected to the church "on the fringe of the core," or that perhaps have one foot in the congregation, one foot in the world.

- Fringe: these are people who likely have no connection with the congregation but are "persons of peace" (Luke 10:7), like the ministers of nearby congregations, local business owners, city officials, school principals, activists, judges, and so on.

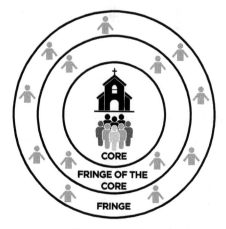

If you don't have a team of people ready to make this journey together, organizing that team could be a good starting point. Here's a couple simple steps to get started.

1. Using the diagram above, discern who is on your team.

2. Make a commitment as a core team to journey together in this experiment for the next six months, perhaps in the form of a simple covenant that each person signs.

3. Identify together who are those "fringe" or "persons of peace" you would like to invite into the conversation.

4. Elect members of the team to make appointments then go and visit these people at work, invite them for a coffee, or attend their worship services.

5. Together decide an appropriate first meeting space for a community listening session, perhaps around a shared meal, and preferably not at your own church facility.

6. During that gathering, lead with listening. Perhaps these two questions could guide the conversation: A. What are the greatest opportunities and needs in this community? B. How might we work together to make our community a better place?

7. Discern together what some simple next steps might be, gather people's contact information, and send out a summary of the time with the next steps you decided.

## "Growing Together"

*Jaidymar A. Smith*
*Laity, Western North Carolina UMC*
*Cultivator, Growing Together*

After my husband and I got married, I moved to North Carolina so that we could start our new chapter together. I remember being excited to move to the United States with my husband. You see, the only time I had been in the United States prior to that was to go to the happiest place on earth, Disney World. Everyone was very friendly, just like they are back home (Puerto Rico). It wasn't long after moving, when I realized people saw me very differently than I was expecting. I remember going to the Farmer's Market on a beautiful, sunny summer morning to help with the family business. While my husband was well known at the market, his wife was not. At first, everyone was so excited to meet the new member of the Smith family. Everything went better than I anticipated, until the very hurtful comments and questions began to crush my heart.

"I am so glad you went there to rescue her. I'm sure she had an awful life down there. That was the Christian thing to do, to bring her here and take her away from the poverty she must have lived in. It must be nice to have someone give you papers that easily allow you to come here. Are you a citizen already? How did you convince him to give you the papers? Are you here legal now? I'm sorry, I cannot understand what you're saying. It's that accent of yours."

I remember being so confused and hurt. As the years go by, I have learned that there is power in sharing your story. Once I began to heal from the hurtful comments, and was able to share my story, and how beautiful my culture is, others began to see that I am not so different from them after all.

A couple of years ago, I was confronted with the concept of assimilation. I had been so hurt and ashamed for being who I was that I automatically assimilated to a culture that was not mine. It was then when I realized that I can be exactly who God created me to be and I could help others do the same. That's when God placed in my heart the idea of having some time to meet with other women, to share our stories, to learn from one another, and to heal together.

"Growing Together" is a Fresh Expression dedicated to women of all ages, languages, cultures, and backgrounds. Every time we meet, we explore our faith and our creativity as we remind ourselves that we are all growing together as we go through this journey called life. We have learned that we don't have to assimilate, but rather live into who God created us to be. It is a safe space for everyone to share their stories while building new connections. It is beautiful to see different languages and cultures together as God intended them to be. But even more powerful is to see how trust has been restored between English-speaking and Spanish-speaking ladies and how relationships have begun to form. God has used creativity as a bridge to unite us.

# Reflection

What strikes you about Jaidymar's story of experiencing racism? What actions can you take to avoid further harm like what she describes? What would healing racialization look like if this story took place in your congregation?

# CHAPTER 2

# Discipleship: Sanctification as Antiracism

*"'Love the Lord your God with all your heart, with all your being, with all your strength, and with all your mind, and love your neighbor as yourself.'"*
*(Luke 10:27 CEB)*

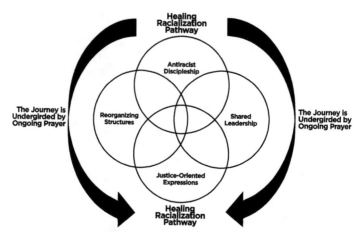

In the *Doing Justice Together: Background & Context* E-Book, available as a companion to this book, we explore the lifelong, grace-centered journey of growing in love with God and neighbor, using John Wesley's well-known analogy of a house. The porch is repentance, the door is faith, and the interior rooms are holiness. Here we want to suggest a process for how teams and congregations can help facilitate the journey of sanctification as an ever-widening circle of love for God and neighbor.

As two ordained United Methodist clergypersons, we live in a Wesleyan expression of the church whose mission statement is "to make disciples of Jesus Christ for the transformation of the world." This holds together two core ideas: works of piety and works of mercy. We are committed to helping people grow in a life of love and faith, and equally committed to how that works out in the world through social justice ministries. Meaning, when we focus on cultivating people who look like Jesus, those people will transform the world through love.

## The Great Omission?

One of the primary scriptures undergirding this mission statement is the Great Commission found in Matthew 28:18-20:

> And Jesus came and said to them, "All authority in heaven and on earth has been given to me. Go therefore and make disciples of all nations, baptizing them in the name of the Father and of the Son and of the Holy Spirit and teaching them to obey everything that I have commanded you. And remember, I am with you always, to the end of the age.

This is a clarion call to *make disciples*, and the fruit of how those disciples transformed the world across the last 2000 years is evident. While the church has at times committed horrible atrocities, it is also the single greatest organized force for good in the world. Christians have fed the hungry, clothed the naked, sheltered strangers, and cared for the vulnerable since the earliest days of the church. They created the first free hospitals, developed orphanages, shelters, and centers of learning. Some Christians fought against slavery, worked for women's equality, and spearheaded the civil rights movement. All of this changed the nature of life, societies, and civilization in remarkable ways.

If you look closely at the UMC mission statement and the Great Commission, you will notice one small but important word is missing from our mission statement: *GO!* Many Methodists across the centuries have interpreted "making disciples" as bringing people into the church building and properly Christianizing them. This is not Jesus's instruction at all.

The Greek word we translate as "go" is πορεύω and is more accurately understood to mean "pursue the journey on which one has entered" or "to continue on one's journey." In the context of our discussion, it might be understood to mean, "as you go on the journey . . . make disciples."

That one little absent word can mean a big change in how people understand their mission. Churches across the denominational spectrum have translated discipleship in terms of butts in pews, nickels and noses, and people attending Bible studies or Sunday school at a building that the congregation usually owns. This is a far cry from the intent of the Great Commission. Jesus envisions a community of learners, going out together, becoming and making disciples as they journey through the normal trials and joys of life. Discipleship is not something that is only happening when we are tucked safely away in the confines of a church compound. Discipleship is happening every moment, every day, and in every encounter of our lives.

## "Make" Disciples?

Another sometimes forgotten aspect is Jesus's promise to be with us always to the end of the age. Here's the rub about "making" disciples: *we can't actually do it.* If we think we can make disciples, we are set up to fail in a massive way. Only the Holy Spirit can make disciples. No person or church can do that. Yet we often act as if we are alone in our efforts, as if Jesus is not always present with us. We can easily slip into the dangerous belief that we somehow bring Jesus with us, or that the Holy Spirit arrives on the scene only after we've arrived ourselves. In this way of thinking, the focus of the action is on us, our efforts, our processes, and our ingenuity.

If we understand prevenient grace, we know that God is working in every space and every human life, long before we get there. God is working in us in ways we are often unaware of. Only the Holy Spirit can do the heavy lifting actually involved in disciple formation. The Spirit woos, awakens, convicts, encourages, and empowers receptive persons to live a transfigured life.

So, what is our role? Perhaps it's creating spaces, processes, and environmental conditions that lend themselves to the Spirit's transformative work?

The New Testament shows a group of flawed and faltering disciples failing forward together on this journey of making disciples. In reality, they were merely continuing the compassionate ministry of Jesus, who ate with sinners (Luke 15:2), healed Gentiles (Luke 7:1-5; Matthew 8:5-13; Mark 7:24-27), and talked with Samaritans, who were considered racially impure and religiously heretical. He shared with them that an age was coming when these points of contention would be made irrelevant and true worshippers would worship in "spirit and truth" (John 4:23). That unorthodox behavior put Jesus at odds with the religious establishment (Matthew 12:1-14), and it later put the disciples in a situation of persecution (Acts 7).

In Acts, the Spirit continues the compassionate work of Jesus. The disciples were transmitting not just a continuation of beliefs and behaviors from the past. They were participating in the emergence of a living, breathing faith taking new shape in the present. After all, Jesus hadn't told them he had given them *all* truth, but that when the Spirit came, he would guide them "in all truth" (John 16:13).

Acts unfolds as a story of the Spirit guiding a flawed and failing group of humans forward into boundary-crossing mission. The Spirit tells Philip to catch up with the eunuch's chariot (8:29) and snatches him away once he's been baptized (8:39). The Spirit pushes Peter past his convictions about what's clean and unclean, telling him in a vision to take and eat (10:13). The Spirit places a vision in Cornelius and initiates the Gentile Pentecost (10:3). The Spirit of Jesus restrains Paul from entering Bithynia (16:7) and inspires him through a vision to travel to Macedonia (16:9).

# Discipleship as Multidimensional

We want to critique several ideas that make discipleship seem one-dimensional. First, the pervasive view of discipleship as *imparting biblical knowledge in a classroom* or sanctuary setting. Instruction is one element of discipleship, teaching us to bend our lives to the truth of scripture, but there is much more.

Second, the emphasis and elevated importance of *our own actions, rather than the Spirit's work*. In this paradigm, we run the risk of playing God.

Third, our eagerness to focus on the Great Commission, before we have spent time with the Great Commandment "to love God and neighbor." We believe these are sequenced in the Bible in this order for a reason. Jesus teaches the disciples to love God and each other under his tutelage through on-the-job training, before sending them out to all the world.

Finally, the tendency to see the Christian life as centered in church facilities, rather than growing as disciples, first, at home with the family; second, at work with colleagues; and third, in places with friends. We too often forget the mobile nature of Jesus's work with the disciples, whom he sends out to do ministry with people. He does *not* tell the disciples to focus on attracting people to the church building.

The pathway we are suggesting here moves us beyond some of this one-dimensional thinking about discipleship. We begin with a focus on working with a small group of people, then explore how to share power, how to cultivate justice-oriented communities, and how to affect the oppressive structures of a racialized society. Each of those dimensions includes aspects of discipleship.

# Learning from Failure

When I (Michael) arrived at a new appointment in a congregation that was known as a clergy-killer, with a history of blatant racism and sexism, I knew I would have my hands full. After consulting with several predecessors, and hearing their stories of clergy abuse, I was terrified. That fear dissipated as I got to know the people and hear their stories.

When I arrive at a new appointment, I seek to visit each member in their homes and my sole intent is to listen, learn, and love. I want to *understand* these people, by *standing-under* their life and their formation as Christians. Typically, I ask three simple questions: 1. What's your story? (and start at the beginning) 2. When did you meet Jesus? 3. What brought you to this church and what are some of your favorite memories? These can be a couple hours long, depending on how forthcoming the congregants are with their lives. In over fifteen years of doing this, I can say that question two usually has the shortest answer, and it is often some version of, "My parents started bringing me to church when I was young . . ." Rarely, can someone describe the moment they met Jesus and, if they can, it often involves a traumatic moment in their lives.

As I was listening to the stories of their lives, sometimes racial slurs, derogatory jokes about persons of color, and even the word "n*gger" were used. One elderly woman highly regarded as a southern saint within the congregation, simply said, "Then the n*ggers came here and it caused . . ." As I learned the history of this place, and that black and brown persons actually inhabited this land before the white settlers showed up, I realized that this church had a culture of white supremacy, and black and brown people were considered the cause of social and economic ills.

I must confess my failure at this point. There were times I did not challenge those racial slurs and portrayals. I knew it was wrong and I failed to act. By doing so I became complicit in perpetuating racism. By not speaking up, I was communicating to them that I was like them. That as a white pastor, I, too, saw persons of color as bad, less than, and a problem. While I do not believe that to be true, I was being a racist, by being a coward.

Unfortunately, this congregation is not an anomaly in the context of North Florida, which has a long history of racism and segregation. Churches have played a significant role in perpetuating this kind of ongoing societal oppression. My tactic was to try and lead with what David

Bosch called "Bold Humility."[4] To let them know I was there to serve them but challenge the evils of racism in direct ways from the Bible through the teaching and preaching ministries of the church. Hindsight being 20/20, that strategy largely failed. If I had had the courage to be forthright and set boundaries making it clear that racist talk was unacceptable in my presence, it could have accelerated the healing of racialization in that community. In the long run, those people left the church anyway, or even more heartbreaking, they died nurturing the poison of racism in their souls.

# Getting Started on the Antiracist Discipleship Journey

Our hope is that your congregation is in a healthier space, one in which people have the spiritual maturity to acknowledge our own racism and complicity in sustaining racist systems.

The first step is to gather a group of people from your church who are willing to engage in a journey of antiracist discipleship. Advertise the beginning of a new study. Invite people to begin reading this book. Or you might begin with a smaller group, your lay leaders or staff, perhaps. Whoever is joining you in this effort, set up regular meetings and begin to work through the questions and reading together. Don't rush it or expect to accomplish ambitious goals in any particular order or time frame. Let the Holy Spirit guide you through the discoveries together over time. You have now begun the journey toward antiracist discipleship.

Putting first things first, we define antiracist discipleship as:

A prayerful process of engagement with biblical and historical sources that helps people and congregations go on a journey of metanoia (a transformation of heart and mind, i.e. repentance) and sanctification. This is a journey of unlearning racist ideas, actions, and policies, to replace them with biblical, antiracist ideas, actions, and polices (Galatians 3:28).

4. Bosch, David J., *Transforming Mission: Paradigm Shifts in Theology of Mission* (Maryknoll, NY: *Orbis Books, 1991*), 390.

## *Metanoia and Sanctification*

Every Christian should be able to identify what repentance has looked like for us. In your gatherings with laity and team members, begin by considering these questions.

What aspects of sin and separation from God have crushed me? How has the kindness of God compelled me to draw closer to him?

We should each be able to articulate, in an open and honest way, what faith looks like for us. What was happening in my life when Jesus invited me to know him?

And most importantly, as people on a journey of sanctification, it is important to consider this question as individuals and as a body: What wounds do we carry into the holy presence of God? Where have we fallen short? Where do we continue to wrestle?

As a team, how can we share and support each other in this journey of sanctification? Can we with transparency answer the question "How goes it with your soul?" And in our responses can we unveil what elements of our ongoing sanctification includes racism? How have we seen that in ourselves? How have we seen it in the systems we inhabit?

## *For Deeper Understanding*

Our e-book, *Doing Justice Together: Background & Context,* offers biblical and historical sources to help your team go on a journey of metanoia and sanctification. It is one tool in the ongoing journey of unlearning racist ideas, actions, and policies, to replace them with biblical, antiracist ideas, actions, and polices. If that sort of journey might be informative, enlightening, or instructive for your team, we suggest you begin your pathway by including that companion resource, as you proceed with the material, questions, and exercises in this book.

The practices suggested at the end of this chapter are designed to help your team move from the porch to the door, using Wesley's analogy, then on to explore the interior rooms together.

# Beginning the Journey

After your team has begun the individual and collective work of repentance, you can take another step. Here, we suggest spending time discussing the concepts of grace and salvation through the Wesleyan lens.

The 12 Steps of recovery fellowships easily harmonize with a Wesleyan way of understanding life as a journey of grace sometimes called the *via salutis*, "way of salvation."[5] At Recovery Church (RC), Michael often has a front-row seat watching how God's transforming and perfecting grace works. RC takes people through the continual movement toward Christian perfection. From "powerless and unmanageable" to "carrying the message and practicing the principles in all affairs" while seeking healing from all "hurts, hang-ups, and habits."[6]

At the soteriological center of our Wesleyan way is the word *grace*. Paul Chilcote notes that the Wesleys "spoke of grace in relational categories."[7] God's intent from the very beginning is to be in relationship with us. As beings created in the image of God (Genesis 1:27), we have the capacity to participate in a loving relationship with God and each other. When we choose sin in our willful rebellion against God and creation, that relationship is broken. Fortunately, in God's grace—God's lavish and unconditional love—God restores us. In Jesus Christ, God does for us what we cannot do for ourselves. We call this great feat of love, *salvation*. Again drawing upon Wesleyan conjunctive theology, salvation is both instantaneous *and* gradual, for salvation is both forgiveness *and* restoration, justification *and* sanctification.

---

5. Maddox, Randy L., *Responsible Grace: John Wesley's Practical Theology* (Nashville: Kingswood Books, 1994), 158.

6. Baker, John, *Celebrate Recovery* (Grand Rapids, MI: Zondervan Publishing House, 2012), 70.

7. Chilcote, Paul, *John & Charles Wesley: Selections from Their Writings and Hymns* (Woodstock, VT: SkyLight Illuminations, 2011), 100.

Dietrich Bonhoeffer reminds us that grace without following Christ is "cheap grace."[8] This is why Christians refer to Jesus not only as our Savior but our Lord, a title that indicates his authority over our lives. God desires that we be holy, as God is holy (1 Peter 1:16). God desires that we live into the fullness of love for God and each other (Luke 10:27). God is quite serious about this. Sanctification is the work God does to restore us from sin and perfect us in love. Randy Maddox highlights the therapeutic nature of Wesleyan theology, which views sin as a "diseased state." We don't just need forgiveness; we need the total healing of our diseased nature.[9]

We often encounter people who emphasize "I got *saved* on this date . . . twenty years ago." Yet, this confines the work of salvation to justification, to the exclusion of the lifelong process of regeneration. Michael uses the disease model in recovery programs, and often reminds folks, "the only thing you can *cure* is a ham." We are all being healed continually one day at a time by the grace of God (Matthew 6:34). We recover, as we continue to yield our broken places and trust in God's strength. God's grace is sufficient, and God's strength is made perfect in our weakness (2 Corinthians 12:9). We are both "saved" *and* "being saved" as we learn to live a life of trust and dependence on God (Acts 2:47; 1 Corinthians 1:18).

Thus, the entire "way of salvation" reveals our Wesleyan theological thrust toward what Maddox calls "responsible grace."[10] God wants to restore us fully to the divine image and enable us to completely love God and neighbor. Yet, this does not occur passively. Our life becomes a lived "response" to God's grace. Our development requires some work on our part. As James reminds us, "faith by itself, if it has no works, is dead" (James 2:17 NRSVUE).

---

8. Furthermore, cheap grace is "grace which amounts to the justification of sin without the justification of the repentant sinner who departs from sin and from whom sin departs." (Bonhoeffer, Dietrich, *The Cost of Discipleship* [New York: Touchstone, 1995], 44.)

9. Maddox, *Responsible Grace*, 82.

10. Ibid., 83.

## The Means of Grace for Disciples

This movement along the "way of salvation" marks our lives in a special way. We grow in both personal and social holiness in this life of grace through the "means of grace."[11] The means of grace are divided into "works of piety" and "works of mercy." Works of piety are focused on personal holiness, including the practices of prayer, fasting, searching the scriptures, and partaking of Holy Communion. Works of mercy are focused on social holiness, including practices of feeding the hungry, clothing the naked, visiting the sick and imprisoned, and working for social justice.[12]

It is through these practices that we are continually infused with God's graceful perfection—holiness of heart and life. We believe with John Wesley that entire sanctification, perfection in love, is achievable in this life. Love of God and neighbor is the ultimate goal, but it cannot be accomplished in isolation. Our very identity as Christians necessitates belonging to a community of accountable discipleship.[13] With our lives now ripe with the fruit of the Spirit (Galatians 5:22-23), we bear the marks of an authentic Christian life, including faith, hope, and love (1 Corinthians 13:13).

A life without spiritual disciplines is a life doomed to disaster. John Wesley suggests his itinerant preachers "Fix some part of every day for private exercises. . . . Whether you like it or no, read and pray daily."[14] The scriptures call all people to a life of spiritual disciplines. These disciplines, based on the practices of Jesus (Luke 5:16; Mark 6:31; Matthew 4:2; Luke 4:16-21), are the practical ways in which we progress in holiness, "love God with all my heart, soul, and mind" and "love neighbor" (see Luke 10:27).

---

11.   Defined as "outward signs, words, or actions, ordained of God, and appointed for this end, to be the ordinary channels [of] grace" (Kinghorn, Kenneth C., *The Standard Sermons in Modern English* [Nashville: Abingdon Press, 2002], 270).

12.   Maddox, 201, 215.

13.   Bonhoeffer, Dietrich, *Life Together* (New York: Harper & Row, 1954), 21.

14.   Harper, Steve, *Devotional Life in the Wesleyan Tradition* (Nashville: Upper Room Books, 1995), 21.

Works of piety and works of mercy give us a framework to heal from the disease of racism. Our individual spiritual growth is hindered by harboring the sin of racism in our hearts.

# The Next Step

In the paragraphs below, you'll find a discipleship framework based on the means of grace to use with your teams as you endeavor to heal from racism. After your team has begun exploring repentance and has deepened their understanding of grace, salvation, and the means of grace for disciples, working through this framework is your next step.

## *Works of Piety*

- Prayer: pray individually and corporately for God to reveal the places where racism is at work. We can regularly acknowledge this sin, confess it, and seek guidance on how to heal it in our lives and community.

  Describe a racist assumption or idea you used to have but no longer do? What was its source? What brought you to the realization that it was wrong? What has repentance looked like?

  Describe how racism has been a part of the history of your congregation? Do you know its origins? What are some ways you might begin to dismantle the structures that have perpetuated it?

- Fasting: we can regularly deny ourselves food or other perceived necessities, as a practice to repent of racism, and grow spiritually to overcome. We will also suggest a form of activistic fasting in the final move of reorganizing structures. What might a set time of fasting and repentance look like for your team? How might you invite the larger congregation to participate? Are there sources (media, books, news networks) of racism that you might commit together to abstain from?

- Bible study: searching the Scriptures, individually and communally, while reading them with a sensitivity to notice what we call racism today and how God instructs us to deal with it.

  Where can we discover examples of what we would today call racism in the Bible? What passages speak against racism? What teachings and actions of Jesus might we consider "anti-racist"? (Use the e-book, *Doing Justice Together: Background & Context* as a guiding resource here).

  Could a Doing Justice Together sermon series and book study be a starting point?

- Holy Communion: as part of the normal flow of repentance, forgiveness, celebration in the Lord's Supper we can include the reality of racialization in the liturgy.

  What would it look like to include a public confession of repentance in the worship experience? Might it be possible to name racism explicitly in the act of confession in the liturgy? For example, "we renounce the spiritual forces of wickedness, which includes the racism in us, and in our world."

## Works of Mercy

- Feeding the hungry: through the ministries aimed at food insecurity, we can ask deeper questions like "how is racialization at play here?" How can we acknowledge how structures caused and sustain these conditions? How can we move from ministries *to* or *for*, to ministries of self-empowerment *with* people experiencing poverty?

- Clothing the naked: through the ministries aimed at providing basic human necessities, we can again ask deeper questions, "like how is racialization at work here?" How can we acknowledge how structures caused and sustain these conditions?

- Visiting the incarcerated and sick: through the ministries aimed at visitation of those experiencing incarceration and illness, we can again ask deeper questions, "like how is racialization fueling this inequity?" How can we acknowledge how structures caused and sustain these conditions? Why are prisons overpopulated with persons of color? Is the healthcare system racially equitable? How would we know?

- Works of mercy prepare us for the works of justice we will discuss later. We can think of works of mercy as treating the symptoms of people who have become deathly sick through drinking poisoned water. Works of justice are discovering the well they've been drinking from and removing the root source of the poisoning itself. We will explore works of justice as the fourth circle—reorganizing structures.

- Story Conversation: Choose one of the audio-video stories provided with this book at the Fresh Expressions channel on Amplify Media[15] and watch or listen together as a team. What strikes you about this person's story of experiencing racism or injustice? Can you make connections with a failure of discipleship within the church at some level? If so describe them?

## "We Are All Equal"

*Jordan Shaw, laity, artist, rapper*
*St Marks, Ocala, FL*

I am sure I began experiencing racism in elementary school but was too young to realize it was racism. I can recall my mother and father saying that this person is being racist. Or they are just being this way because we are black. But the first time I can recall experiencing racism personally,

15.   https://my.amplifymedia.com/freshexpressions/home

was when I was in middle school. There was a Caucasian girl in my class, she liked me, and I really liked her. So, we decided we would be boyfriend and girlfriend. We started hanging out every day after school, and she would even wear my football jersey on Fridays. We really enjoyed spending time with each other. I would go to her house, and we would just sit in the yard and talk.

One day her little sister told her parents that a black boy had been coming to their house. Her dad got my phone number, called my house, and told my mother that I was not allowed to be around his daughter, and that "his daughter is not allowed to hang out with boys that are not the same race as her." My mother told him he had nothing to worry about and that he would never see me at their house again. While my mother did not agree with him, she was afraid of what may happen to me if he caught me at his house. I never saw my girlfriend again. When I got to school the next day, she had withdrawn from school, and I was told she and her family were moving to Kentucky. I was crushed. I have always been sociable and excelled in school and athletics. I had never experienced someone openly disliking me just because of the color of my skin.

That experience left scars. It has stayed with me for the rest of my life. That situation made me feel like I always had to keep my guard up, and that I must read the room before I feel welcome to stay. When I walked into St. Marks United Methodist Church, Ocala, at first, I was a little weary. I was the only African American in the room. But soon I felt totally at ease as I was welcomed with open arms. Leading up to the visit, I had connected with people from St. Marks at a diverse gathering called Higher Power Hour, a fresh expression that meets in the chemical dependency unit of a local rehabilitation facility. There, I was shown only support and respect. I now co-lead that gathering.

At St Marks everyone is taught to love thy neighbor, and you can feel that energy in the room. Now, as an artist and rapper, I regularly perform my original songs in the main worship services. The people are always so grateful and affirming. My relationship with God today has taught me to never pass judgement and to accept people for who they are. I've realized that I can't judge all white people based on the experiences of racism I've endured. With that being said I hope to be an example to others, to show that *we are all equal.*

# Reflection

What strikes you about Jordan's experience of racism at a young age and how it impacted his life? What actions could you take to make your community look like a welcoming space where "we are all equal"? What would healing racialization look like if this story took place in your congregation?

CHAPTER 3

# Shared Leadership

*When Pentecost Day arrived, they were all together in one place.*
*(Acts 2:1 CEB)*

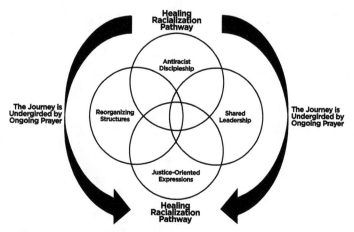

The outpouring of the Spirit at Pentecost was one of the most transformative moments in human history. Afterward, Peter, empowered by the Spirit, begins to preach. He points to its significance as being fulfilled by the prophet Joel…

Rather, this is what was spoken through the prophet Joel:

> In the last days, God says,
> I will pour out my Spirit on all people.
> > Your sons and daughters will prophesy.
> > Your young will see visions.
> > Your elders will dream dreams.
> > Even upon my servants, men and women,

> I will pour out my Spirit in those days,
> and they will prophesy.
> I will cause wonders to occur in the heavens above
> and signs on the earth below,
> blood and fire and a cloud of smoke.
> The sun will be changed into darkness,
> and the moon will be changed into blood,
> before the great and spectacular day of the Lord comes.
> And everyone who calls on the name of the Lord will be saved.
> (Acts 2:16-21 CEB)

We noted earlier the miraculous nature of God pouring out the Spirit "upon all flesh," not just a select few anointed ones, but every*body*. We considered how this new reality includes the fact that women and men "shall prophesy," and the normal constraints of age will be transformed, young people will have visionary foresight and wisdom, and older people will not lose the capacity to dream. We suggested even the economic and social caste systems are flipped, slaves are no longer at the bottom of the invisible pyramid but are equally empowered. The barriers of sexism have also been reversed, "both men and women," have received this outpouring, and they can supernaturally function in the gifts of the Spirit.

Here we want to focus on the distributed nature of Pentecost as a manifestation of *shared leadership*.

# Pentecost Power

At Pentecost, the "power" Jesus promised (Acts 1:8) was poured out in an equalizing, adaptive, and collectivistic way. The power was distributed throughout the entire community. It expands like an ever-widening circle. "All" of the disciples were empowered and gifted as a community of equals, with a clear missional focus (Acts 2:4). The "power" was shared, relational, decentralized, and self-organized. This enabled the disciples to spread the love of Jesus from "Jerusalem, in all Judea and Samaria, and to the end of the earth" (Acts 1:8). Jesus's ascension is not just about where

Jesus goes; it is also about where Jesus leaves. For the disciples to be Jesus's body on earth, Jesus's physical body had to leave to make room for the disciples to become his new embodiment.

A racialized church has largely failed to continue this shared power dynamic as a diverse community of equals. The multiethnic church movement has made a valiant attempt at cultivating congregations that look like Acts 2, but we have fallen short. We seem to have failed to take into account the structural reality of the invisible pyramid.

Oneya Okuwobi documents the failure of the multiethnic church movement to fully empower leaders of color. She calls it "the failure of shared leadership" and writes, "Without a change in leadership, there can't exist the knowledge and commitment necessary to create equitable spaces for all congregants."[16] A strange form of leadership and fascination with power, alien to the way of Jesus, seems to have corrupted the church in many ways. So how do we heal this wound?

# Circles Not Pyramids

The Trinity is a paradigm for shared leadership. Who is the leader in the triune God? The dynamic relational nature of the Father, Son, and Spirit contrasts starkly with the static hierarchies we so often see embedded in the church. In the triune God, we see relational movement and a dance of leadership. The Trinity is not a hierarchy, with one person in authority over the other persons, but an interactive, nonlinear, relational community.

*Perichoresis*, the relational dance of mutual indwelling, is not about one person of the Trinity ruling over the others. It is a shared mode, each making room for the other, each taking the lead of the divine dance at different times.

This image of shared leadership sits in stark contrast to the type of leadership we see across the ages in the church. In fact, the ways we have

---

16. Oneya Okuwobi, "Moving Forward on Race," in *Red Skies: 10 Essential Conversations Exploring Our Future as the Church.*

conceived and practiced leadership have often been deeply harmful. People in positions of power are prone to abuse power. Diane Langberg highlights how "We seem to ground authority in position or gender and then require obedience to that authority. But all authority is Christ's, and any derivative of that power given to us is to be submitted to him in love."[17] We can look back over the course of church history, recent and modern, and see how power has often played out in destructive ways and has too infrequently resembled the trinitarian model or the example of Christ.

## Leadership as Relationship

Leadership is a relational phenomenon that occurs through synergistic interactions between the persons in a community.

Systems theorist Edwin Friedman highlighted the fact that true adaptation is the work of the people. We have often interpreted leadership through an individualistic lens. The heroic leader acts upon and saves the system, by singlehandedly carrying it on her or his shoulders. In reality, a leader guides a process in which the people with the problem internalize the change for themselves. At different times, diverse members of the community will offer leadership as the need arises.[18]

The church has used this hierarchal view of leadership in many self-defeating ways. In the heroic solo leader model, the emphasis is placed on extrinsic motivation. The leader offers a compelling vision and charges a community to follow him or her to take the hill. Members of the community are encouraged to remember the "vision statement" as a kind of sacred mantra. They are to internalize the vision and let it be an external motivator. In our experience, this kind of approach is rarely successful.

Shared leadership requires helping people find intrinsic motivation. The leader helps people discern what is going on in their interior life. What wakes us up in the morning? What energizes us? What keeps us up

---

17.   Langberg, Diane, *Redeeming Power: Understanding Authority and Abuse in the Church* (Ada, MI: Brazos Press, 2020), 122.

18.   Edwin H. Friedman, *A Failure of Nerve: Leadership in the Age of the Quick Fix* (New York: Seabury Press, 2007), 54.

at night? What broke us? What wicked problem do we see in the world? What is so beautiful that it compels us to act even in adverse circumstances? What gifts, graces, and skills do we possess? A key question here is "What is God calling me to do?" Then, how does that personal calling intersect with the larger mission of the community. This is partly why in the next chapter we will advocate for a Fresh Expressions approach that flows from intrinsic motivation and brings together an orientation toward social justice.

The individualistic renderings of leadership long accepted within the church have been largely discredited within the field of complexity thinking. Leadership is an emergent process that involves a series of synergistic relational interactions. Each agent in the system can act in ways that change the trajectory of an organization, for better or for worse. When power is overly concentrated with one actor, it creates more potential for harm. Thus, a quick survey of Christian history shows where this has gone wrong: scandals, abuse, cover-ups, and a trail of victims left in the wake.

If we take our cues from the relational nature of the Trinity, relationships are not designed to be organized hierarchically. Relationships should be organized in circles, not pyramids. Further, if we study the ministry of the disinherited Jesus, he was often in conflict with the agents at the top of a power hierarchy. He critiqued their use of power, how it excluded and marginalized the very people they were supposed to be caring for (Matthew 23).

## In the Name *and* Way of Jesus

Jesus intentionally chose disciples at the bottom of the invisible pyramid. Not religious professionals or educated elites, but everyday laborers, fishermen, tax collectors, and people with a checkered past. He organized the community in a shared leadership way. He equipped the disciples to do what he was doing and then gave them feedback as they went along. He invited their feedback and they felt comfortable within this shared leadership dynamic even to push back on some of his core ideas (Matthew 16:21-27). The disciples were empowered by the Spirit to embody that kind of community following his ascension and Pentecost.

Clearly, Jesus prepared the disciples to step into leadership functions (Matthew 16:21-23), with the expectation that they would not only continue his ministry but do even "greater works" with the coming empowerment of the Spirit (John 14:12). However, they wrestled to embody the kind of shared leadership community Jesus taught them to be, defaulting back to old hierarchical models and racist assumptions (Acts 10–11). Yet it is telling that even those outside the core founding group felt comfortable enough to challenge the most influential in the group, Paul and his conflicts with Peter for example (Galatians 2:11-13).

We don't want to minimize the role of leadership itself, but rather offer a critique of the dominant version of leadership, which is not shared, not equitable, and causes harm.

The leadership ideology that has been pervasive in the Western church is in part responsible for preserving racialization. This is why we believe that the church has not gone far enough. The desire to create multiethnic congregations is noble and a great start down the path of healing racialization. But hierarchical forms of leadership have historically suppressed the voices and gifts of persons of color. That is leadership in the name of Jesus, but not in the way of Jesus. When the church functions in this way we do harm.

Communities committed to shared leadership can go about ministry in the name of Jesus *and in the way of Jesus.*

# Structured for Racism

The United Methodist Social Principles state, "Racism, manifested as sin, plagues and hinders our relationship with Christ, inasmuch as it is antithetical to the gospel itself. . . . We commit as the Church to move beyond symbolic expressions and representative models that do not challenge unjust systems of power and access."[19] We are sure that if you've read this far that you can say a big "amen!" to this. But what do we actually do? How do we actually move beyond "symbolic expressions and representative models" and actually challenge unjust systems of power and access? And how do we do this from the setting of our local congregations?

We believe the lack of racial equality regarding shared leadership can be traced back to racist structures and polity. In some ways we are structured for racism.

The features of structural racism are still embedded in denominations today, witnessed by the disparities in salary, opportunity, and available appointments to healthy churches. Even in congregations that are seeking to embody a multiethnic culture, it's often white leaders in key positions of power. Those leaders make decisions and act upon the system from a hierarchical vantage point. For instance, it is their vision to have a multicultural church. They are key influencers in the selection of staff, and their termination. They guide the boards or committees to make decisions together, but often those groups serve a perfunctory purpose. The leader's will is often and ultimately done.

In these uneven power dynamic scenarios, racial minority staff are expected to perform at levels superior to white counterparts. They are expected to agree with organizational decisions with little feedback into the system. They are often compensated unequally in comparison to their white counterparts.

There is also a significant possibility of tokenism which again refers to the practice of making only a symbolic effort to recruit and platform persons of a racial minority to give the illusion of equality. A key concept in the multicultural church movement is to "have diversity on the stage." The question we want to pose is this . . . Is there also diversity in the boardroom? Meaning, are persons of color seated as equals around the table where organizational decisions are made? Are they given a

19. *Social Principles: The Social Community*, 2016. https://www.umc.org/en/content/social-principles-the-social-community, accessed November 25, 2023.

shared opportunity to guide and shape the culture and decisions of the organization?

This requires local churches to do away with pyramids and replace them with round tables. It also takes humility, courage, and high trust in the Holy Spirit.

## Can We Change Our Ways?

In many cases, this will require internal reorganization. Can a senior leader live without the title "senior" in front of their name? Can multiple clergy congregations be a team of co-pastors, rather than seniors and associates? Can church boards reflect the diversity they hope to see "on the stage" and in the congregation? Does the leadership team have the courage to do a racial salary audit and ensure there is equitable compensation across the board? Can entire denominations take this kind of a stance?

There can only truly be multiethnic congregations when there are multiethnic shared power dynamics. While this may be attempted through staffing in the case of larger churches, we have seen this play out in smaller and midsized congregations with no staff as well.

We realize this is hard work that can't take place overnight. The starting point could be antiracist discipleship that helps people see the invisible pyramid. But then it must empower those same people to deconstruct that pyramid together.

We have noted previously that one persistent facet of this system is economic. Keri Day demonstrates how neoliberal capitalism is the overarching structure that preserves this inequity. She writes, "Our religious and moral imaginations are imprisoned to the fundamental market rationality of atomic individualism, which makes questions of caring relations seem idealistic and even naïve. We are often unable to imagine deeper modes of social connectedness or cooperation, as the grid of social intelligence that neoliberalism offers us is based on the pessimistic premise of radical individual self-interest."[20]

Can the church alter an alternative vision of communal life apart from atomic individualism? Can we imagine and embody new and deeper modes of connectedness and cooperation? How might we begin to create these communities of shared empowerment?

# A Taste of Grace

For Michael, trying to change the culture of an all-white congregation with deep roots in slavery, racism, and segregation from the inside was nearly impossible. Through co-organizing antiracism marches and planting a small expression of church in the Martin Luther King Jr. building, he began to form a bundle of relationships that embodied a shared power dynamic. The pastors and churches involved began to invite each other to joint worship experiences and revivals where each leader played a role.

The groups began to have meals together where each person shared about their life journey and why they were a part of the group. Over time they deepened those relationships and learned to trust one another. The congregations witnessed this shared power dynamic and were invited into it. But things really turned the corner when one of the black pastors was interested in moving his church plant into the all-white Wildwood congregation's facility.

This would require board approval, and so the team began to pray and seek the Lord. They were given a scripture to open the first meeting, "Because we loved you so much, we were delighted to share with you not only the gospel of God but our lives as well" (1 Thessalonians 2:8 NIV). In a heated board meeting, it was proposed not only that they wanted to allow the church plant to move in, but that there should be no monetary arrangement, and that key leaders of the church plant should be invited to sit on the board as equals. Providing the space for free was a way to make

---

20.    Day, Keri, *Religious Resistance to Neoliberalism: Womanist and Black Feminist Perspectives* (Houndmills, Basingstoke, Hampshire, UK: Palgrave Macmillan, 2015), 12.

reparations for past harm and heal the blemish of racism in the history of the church. By inviting leaders to serve as trustees, it would give them an equal voice in how the congregations moved forward together.

There was a considerable amount of pushback with some leaders storming out of the meeting. Ultimately, there was enough of a majority vote to move forward. There is nothing wrong with financial contracts around congregations sharing space, but in this scenario it was contextually appropriate to proceed not in a contractual agreement but in a kingdom partnership. We realize those things are not mutually exclusive either, but in this case, it was the right thing to do. This did cause an exodus of long-term members. Some who were committed to the conviction that "they have their church, and we have ours, we shouldn't be mixing the two." One of them called the Beck's biracial granddaughter a "half-breed" and stated they "shouldn't be mixing the species."

Next, these two diverse congregations attempted to hold joint worship services. The result was essentially disastrous. Both the majority of the white members, and black members, were dissatisfied. Both groups felt like combining was in some way diminishing the distinct cultures that were expressed in worship. A black Pentecostal church and a white Methodist church don't necessarily go about worship in the same way. So together, the leadership made a decision to continue worshipping separately on Sunday mornings, but to create a new communal gathering together on Wednesday nights. This was called Taste of Grace, a dinner church, in which worship was centered around Jesus and a shared meal. Here was a universal exercise that both congregations could agree upon . . . eating good food![21]

Yet Taste of Grace was more than a community dinner, it became an instrument of reconciliation. The community was a thin space, where people could experience healing from the trauma of racism.

Judith Herman, in her seminal work *Trauma and Recovery* writes, "Because the traumatic syndromes have basic features in common, the

---

21.    See more about Taste of Grace here:  (59) "Taste of Grace" Dinner Church - YouTube.

recovery process also follows a common pathway. The fundamental stages of recovery are establishing safety, reconstructing the trauma story, and restoring the connection between survivors and their community."[22] They didn't realize it at the time, but the community dinner was creating a context for this kind of healing.

In cultivating shared-power communities of healing, three primary ingredients are required, they must be: safe, accessible, and real. Safe: places of healing, not harm, environments of grace, inclusive spaces where all were welcome and where "good news" is truly good and truly made available to all (Luke 4:18-19). Accessible: meaning close, in our normal living space and rhythm, and speaking a common language all can understand, just as Jesus did when he came and made his dwelling among us (John 1:14). Real: people can be honest about their real wounds. They can process their pain in an unfiltered way with uncensored language, a prayerful articulation that brings real healing (James 5:16).[23]

We consider the early Methodist movement as an example of these kinds of communities. Those first communities were places of embodied hospitality. They were places of healing because they were safe, accessible, and real.

- Safe: The communities met in smaller, intimate groups. All people from every social status were welcome, and equally empowered. Harmful behaviors were not tolerated.

- Accessible: The communities were formed in the normal spaces where people gathered and spoke what has been described as "plain truth for plain people." The only requirement for membership was a desire to grow spiritually.

- Real: People were invited to come to terms with and express their brokenness. Methodist small groups asked, "How goes it with your soul?" People were invited to name their

---

22. Herman, Judith L., *Trauma and Recovery: The Aftermath of Violence—From Domestic Abuse to Political Terror* (New York: Basic Books, 1992), 3.

23. Beck, Michael, *Painting with Ashes: When Your Weakness Becomes Your Superpower* (Plano, TX: Invite Press, 2022), 48.

woundedness in a community of reciprocity and mutual support.[24]

Each week at Taste of Grace, as people sat together and learned each other's names and stories, different members of the community were invited to stand up and give a testimony or share a Jesus Story. Often in that space of testimony, people would acknowledge their woundedness and pain.

## Circles That Heal

From an Africentric perspective this created a circle of communal healing. In many Western schools of therapy, the paid professional often guides the client toward individuation, self-realization, and a well-developed ego. However, African therapeutic modalities include testimony therapy, which focuses on sharing in a collective story. Testimony therapy is communitarian and social constructionist in nature. It is grounded in the concept of Ubuntu—if we are persons through other persons our healing will most powerfully manifest in community with others.

For example, in the black church where Stephanie grew up, testify'n is a ritual in which members of the community "share their testimony." The narrative includes an honest articulation of some struggle or pain, followed by the pivot often captured by the words "but God . . ." It was hard, but God brought me through. I went through a struggle, but God was faithful. The community participates through call-and-response in the individual's story with "go ahead," "tell it," "make it plain," and "amen."[25]

When people shared their story at Taste of Grace, they were journeying through a therapeutic process that brought healing in the context of community. Many in the community were experiencing marginalization,

---

24. Beck, Michael, *Painting with Ashes*, 31.

25. Akinyela, Makungu M., "Testimony of Hope: African Centered Praxis for Therapeutic Ends," *Journal of Systemic Therapies* 24.1 (2005): 5-18. https://www.academia.edu/2324704 /Testimony_of_hope_African_centered_praxis_for_therapeutic_ends. Accessed November 26, 2023.

denied access to some of the more exclusive (and expensive) Western healing modalities employed by individualistic cultures. This resource for
communal healing was free and accessible for all. This method of healing
individual and collective trauma is closely aligned with the collectivistic
culture of the Hebrew people and the tradition of lament.

As Judith Herman notes, "To hold traumatic reality in consciousness
requires a social context that affirms and protects the victim and that joins
victim and witness in a common alliance. For the individual victim, this
social context is created by relationships with friends, lovers, and family.
For the larger society, the social context is created by political movements
that give voice to the disempowered."[26]

Taste of Grace ultimately became a justice-oriented expression of
church. It served to re-ligament people once fragmented by racist ideas
and assumptions in a common alliance. It gave space for those who felt
silenced to speak. It silenced those often privileged to speak without con-
straint, placing them in a posture of listening. It became a vehicle to empower those who felt disempowered by the racist structures.

Taste of Grace began to employ the four healing questions from testimony therapy as a guide:

1. What happened to you?
2. How does what happened to you affect you now?
3. What do you need to heal?
4. In spite of what happened to you, what gives you strength to
   go on?

The church is Jesus's plan for the healing of the world. These are justice-oriented communities that embody his own life. So, one of the most
essential and restorative things we can possibly do is cultivate new forms
of church where we can experience healing. These must be communities
of mutual empowerment.

---

26.  Herman, Judith, 9.

This community dinner was formed through the commitment to shared leadership. But it was also missional in purpose. From the outset, Taste of Grace was focused on those not currently connected to the churches. Wildwood has a large food pantry that serves hundreds of families each week. The team of people, black and white, began to pass out fliers to the regulars of the pantry inviting them to a free community dinner.

The team entered into a journey of self-emptying by laying aside assumptions and adventuring out together into a new space. As they immersed themselves in the neighborhood, listening to the hopes and struggles of the people, they felt there was a pain-point around food insecurity. They pooled their resources, time, talents, and treasures, to create something together that would counter the economic inequity in the community. Food insecurity manifested in a particularly inequitable way for persons of color.

Elaine Heath writes, "One model of kenosis for today could be small, missional congregations led by teams of bivocational pastors."[27] Unbeknownst to them at the time, WildOnes were creating exactly this kind of community together and learning from each other new ways of being the church. They also discovered together these communities could break free of the normative economic patterns.

## Becoming a Beloved Community

They didn't realize it at the time, but in partnering together to create a justice-oriented expression, their own relationships were deepened. They were becoming a beloved community through their work of doing justice together. In the next chapter we will explore a framework for creating these kinds of communities.

For Wildwood, this new form of church served to facilitate a therapeutic journey as people sat around tables as learners of each other. People with long-standing racial prejudices began to humanize their "racial other."

27. Heath, Elaine A., *The Mystic Way of Evangelism: A Contemplative Vision for Christian Outreach* (Grand Rapids, MI: Baker Academic, 2017), 87.

Leadership of the new experience was shared by each church equally. Each week, both laity and clergy provided the diverse testimonies and facilitated the healing questions. The group talked at their tables about the questions and shared insights with the larger body. They discovered over time, as people really connected and got to know each other, they were more comfortable adapting their own traditions to worship together.

This new arrangement unlocked a prayerful process of sharing power, in which persons of color took up equal positions of leadership throughout the congregation/organization. This began to dismantle the assumptions of white supremacy built into the white congregation and challenged racist assumptions persons of color had about the whites. Because power was distributed evenly among the whole community, more and more laity felt comfortable participating and leading. Mixed race task-teams started working together to plan more fellowship events and unity marches.

As equals in decision making, the superficial nature often associated with congregations in the multicultural movement was dismantled. This enabled the congregations to abolish mere tokenism, and really learn to live, love, lead, and make decisions together as a body.

## A Beacon of Hope

In 2023, the community removed together a historic plaque of the congregation's genesis as a Methodist Episcopal South church planted in 1882. The marker was located at the foot of the church bell tower, a kind of enduring symbol of racism and segregation. Local news outlets ran stories when the trustees destroyed the plaque with a sledgehammer. Now the bell tower is a beacon of hope to the community. Today it symbolizes the possible healing of racialization that can take place when the people commit to share power. It's an icon pointing to a body of believers, equally filled with the Spirit, who reflect the togetheversity of that first Pentecost. A community of people committed to *doing justice together*.

# The Next Step

In the exercise below, you'll find a shared leadership framework based on the ideas in this chapter. Gather your team to work through the exercises together.

- Draw a pyramid on a white board or stick-up paper. In your congregation, who is at the top of the leadership hierarchy? Who is at the bottom? List each committee, team, and leader, locating them somewhere on the pyramid. What problems do you see with the structure? For instance, can God only speak/work through the people at the top?

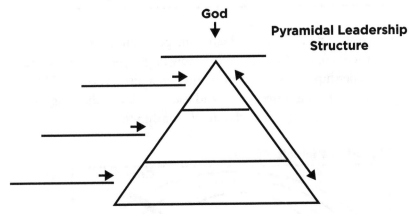

- Now consider the relational circles and shared leadership way of Jesus himself. It seems that Jesus had people who lived in greater degrees of intimacy and followership. Some like the female disciples who traveled along with him providing out of their own means (Lk 8:1-3), Lazarus, Martha, and Mary in Bethany (Jn 11:5), Peter, James, and John who were present for significant healings and the transfiguration (Mark 5:37, 14:33). Yet there were also the 12 core disciples (Lk 6:12-13), the 72 sent on mission (Lk 10:1), and the 120 who gathered at Pentecost (Acts 2:4). As he impacted these disciples deeply, they in turn interacted with the crowds and ultimately the entire world. What do you notice about the relational and shared leadership way of Jesus? How is it different than a pyramid?

**Jesus's Relational Circles**

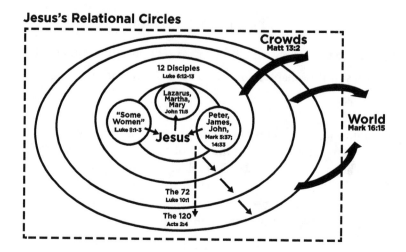

- Now using the diagram below, imagine your congregation as a series of overlapping circles. How might you reorganize the leadership structures of the church in a distributed way? Using each committee, team, and leader, redesign the congregation as a series of circles in relationship to Jesus.

**Shared Leadership Circles**

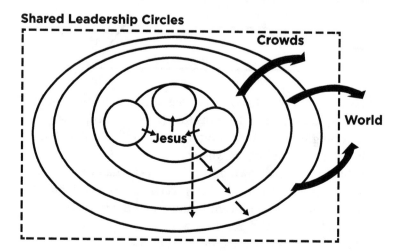

- This chapter suggested "diversity on the stage" can be a form of tokenism when there is not "diversity in the board room." Use the following questions to assess the diversity of your congregation.

- What is the racial makeup of your congregation?
- How many persons of color serve in leadership positions?
- How many persons of color serve as paid staff?
- Is there equity in the compensation?
- Are persons of color equals in decision making "in the board room"?
- What possible next steps could further move your congregation towards a culture of racial equity and shared leadership?

# "One Coffee, One Conversation at a Time"

*Tracy Rose Midweek Grind*
*Tallahassee, FL*

I was raised in the church, predominantly the Baptist denomination. I realized I was part of the LGBTQIA+ community early on. But I was in my early twenties when I finally became honest with everyone else about who I was. I went to the church I was attending and talked with the pastor about it. I was told that I was not welcome there if that is how I felt. Very long story short, I moved to another state, got divorced, and began church hopping.

I would often find a church I liked, connected with the people, etc. but inevitably someone would find out I was LGBTQIA+ and I would be told I couldn't serve in the church. Or I couldn't serve in any way that involved children. I was shunned/ostracized within the church itself, or straight up asked to leave. This went on for a while until I was so hurt that I left the church altogether. I spent five years of my life re-reading the Bible through a new lens, studying, praying, reading, interpreting, and reading some more. It was just me and God for those five years and it took that long for me to begin to heal and for God to undo the damage that the church had done to me. Finally, God told me that God did not have a problem with my sexuality. There was work for me to do inside the church and I needed to get busy doing it.

I stumbled into Good Samaritan UMC by way of a persistent but gentle invitation from a friend to come check it out. I fell in love with the church immediately and when I walked through the doors it was as if God said, welcome home—your work begins here. I spoke with the pastor at the time who assured me that I was welcome to serve in any capacity and so I jumped in. Then the infamous vote happened at the 2019 General Conference that retained restrictions against "self-avowed practicing homosexuals." I wanted to run but I sensed God saying no—you have work to do here. You are a bridge. You are going to help bridge the gap between the church world and the LGBTQIA+ world. You are going to help me, help them figure out that they are all my beautiful children and I love them all equally. And the more difficult work—they need to love each other as I love them.

I began my Fresh Expressions journey that same year. In November or so of 2022 God called me to start a Fresh Expression, to begin it in January of 2023, and to center it around the things in life I am passionate about. Jesus, coffee, people, and conversation. So, we launched Midweek Grind, a beautiful expression of what it looks like to do life with each other with no judgment for where each of us are or what our individual beliefs are. We exist to brew a safe space for the LGBTQIA+ community and allies to gather and talk about life and faith and what that looks like for each of us. We do this understanding we are all on our own journey, no one's journey is the same, but knowing we, as a community, can support each other. And we do this one cup of coffee and one conversation at a time.

# Reflection

What strikes you about Tracy's story of experiencing marginalization and exclusion? What simple actions can you take to avoid further harm like what she describes? What would healing look like if this story took place in your congregation? What small experiment might you begin with, something like Midweek Grind?

# CHAPTER 4

# Justice-Oriented Expressions

*"Whenever you enter a city and its people welcome you, eat what they set before you. Heal the sick who are there, and say to them, 'God's kingdom has come upon you.'"*
(Luke 10:8-9 CEB)

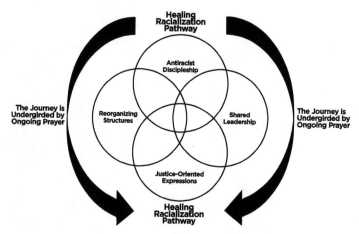

In the Western church, we have dichotomized church planting and social justice. Church planters are thought to be apostolically gifted individuals who venture into uncharted territory to start a new faith community. Those involved in social justice are typically prophetic, social activists, leading movements that seek to create a world that is more equitable and just. It's thought that these two activities are distinct and separate, requiring leaders with different gifts and passions.

There are several flaws in this thinking. First, the individualistic view of leaders. We envision these leaders as a kind of superhuman, keystone species in the ecclesial space. They possess unusual gifts and capacities, to be used in these extraordinary callings primarily outside the current inherited church. This approach is unhelpful and can cause harm, especially when leaders abuse their power. It is also harmful to the soul of the leader if they see themselves as the primary actor doing God's work on behalf of God. No one can carry that load for long, we aren't meant to.

# Reconciling Evangelism, Social Justice, and Church Planting

Another flaw lies in the collapsed understanding of evangelism, justice, and salvation. Those words describe distinct concepts, but they are also inextricably intertwined. Jesus came heralding the inbreaking of God's kingdom in a fresh way. He goes to the synagogue in Nazareth, he reads from the scroll of Isaiah, and says,

> "The Spirit of the Lord is upon me,
> because the Lord has anointed me.
> He has sent me to preach good news to the poor,
> to proclaim release to the prisoners
> and recovery of sight to the blind,
> to liberate the oppressed,
> and to proclaim the year of the Lord's favor."
> (Luke 4:18-19)

You could call this the moment when Jesus publicly declares his personal mission statement. He tells the people there that day, essentially, "I am the fulfillment of these words." Jesus goes about doing those exact things, but he does so in the context of planting a church, his church. He begins to collect a group of misfits and everyday folks from the non-religious elites. His disciple group is revolutionary in its diversity . . . men and women!

**49**

And fishermen, tax collectors, zealots, sex workers, and other people who had questionable pasts.

As he goes about embodying Isaiah's social justice litany, he is also creating a community. He empowers his teams to embody Isaiah's litany, too. Consider Luke 9:1-6 (CEB):

> Jesus called the Twelve together and he gave them power and authority over all demons and to heal sicknesses. He sent them out to proclaim God's kingdom and to heal the sick. He told them, "Take nothing for the journey—no walking stick, no bag, no bread, no money, not even an extra shirt. Whatever house you enter, remain there until you leave that place. Wherever they don't welcome you, as you leave that city, shake the dust off your feet as a witness against them." They departed and went through the villages proclaiming the good news and healing people everywhere.

We can see that the Twelve become an extension of Jesus's own ministry. They have been given "power and authority" that is shared and distributed among them. They are announcing the breaking in of the kingdom of God, accompanied by healing and liberation. They are literally doing what Jesus is doing, now multiplied by twelve. There is not just one Jesus now, but a dozen of them (and the women that so often go unnamed, Luke 8:1-3), embodying what Jesus declared he would do back in the synagogue in Nazareth.

As Leonardo Boff states, "Now we can say that Jesus did not select the Twelve as founders of future churches. Jesus established the Twelve as a community: as messianic, eschatological church. The apostles are not to be understood first and foremost as individuals, but precisely as the Twelve, as messianic community gathered around Jesus and his Spirit. This community then broadened and gave rise to other apostolic communities."[28]

Now here we might pause and say, "Well yes, but aren't these twelve a select group of uniquely called and gifted individuals?"

Let's move forward to Luke 10 . . .

---

28. Boff, Leonardo, *Ecclesiogenesis: The Base Communities Reinvent the Church* (Maryknoll, NY: Orbis Books, 1985), 25.

> After these things, the Lord commissioned seventy-two others and sent them on ahead in pairs to every city and place he was about to go. He said to them, "The harvest is bigger than you can imagine, but there are few workers. Therefore, plead with the Lord of the harvest to send out workers for his harvest. Go! Be warned, though, that I'm sending you out as lambs among wolves. Carry no wallet, no bag, and no sandals. Don't even greet anyone along the way. Whenever you enter a house, first say, 'May peace be on this house.' If anyone there shares God's peace, then your peace will rest on that person. If not, your blessing will return to you. Remain in this house, eating and drinking whatever they set before you, for workers deserve their pay. Don't move from house to house. Whenever you enter a city and its people welcome you, eat what they set before you. Heal the sick who are there, and say to them, 'God's kingdom has come upon you.' " (verses 1-9 CEB)

Not only are the Twelve given power and authority to do what Jesus is doing, but the entire community of disciples is now sent out. There's not just twelve . . . there are seventy-two of them! Remember, the term *Christian* literally denotes a "little Christ," and these seventy-two are embodying the ministry of Jesus himself.

As we explore these passages, pause and consider what Jesus didn't do. He did not get a group of folks together and build a house of worship. He did not stick up a sign and tell people where to meet him on Sundays at 9 and 11am. He did not send out disciples as heroic-solo leaders, but in teams of at least two. He was out on the move with the disciples moving place to place. He did not hold some of the disciples back at the compound to pray and wait. He did not tell them to go and "take" and "make" and "build." He sent them in a posture of vulnerability, with the few items they had on a journey of faith to locate the "persons of peace."

This is a posture of mutuality—you will find a person there who welcomes you. A person who opens their table to you. A person who feeds you. A person who helps you establish yourself in the community. A person who you will stay with, not moving around house to house, but abiding with as long as they will have you. You need them and what they provide, just as much as they need you. Once all of that relational activity takes place, once you know them and are known by them, then preach, heal, and herald the arrival of the kingdom. Then you can proclaim good news to the poor, proclaim freedom for the prisoners, recovery of sight for the blind, and set the oppressed free.

Jesus does not disconnect the work of evangelism, justice, and church planting. It is through the creation of this new community that those things manifest. As you heal, as you release, as you do justice together, you are planting the church. As you do this, you are liberating the oppressed, setting the captives free. And those tasks are not the work of specialists, they are the work of the whole people of God—together.

For Jesus, social justice, the liberation and healing of marginalized and disinherited peoples was the forethought, the purpose, the why. The church was designed to facilitate that transformation. A community that embodied the kingdom of God, was the method. In the dominating Christendom model, social justice was largely an afterthought. It was something we might get around to after all the important work of church planting and Christianizing was done. We could train specialists to do the extracurricular activities of the church, like healing the sick, liberating captives, and feeding the hungry.

For Jesus, evangelism was embodying the good news in word and deed. Evangelism led to healing, shalom, and the restoration of relationships. It was not about convincing someone to believe a proposition that kept them from hell when they die. It was about liberating disinherited people from the hell in which they were already living. Discipleship was the spiritual formation that took place during this activity. Jesus showed the disciples what to do. They did it. Then he said, "Let's talk about how you could do that differently or better." The church came into being through the process of organizing life around the priorities and actions of Jesus. Churches should still come into being that way. Indeed, they are, all over the world through movements like the Base Ecclesial Communities and Fresh Expressions.

It's easy to trace the history of where these separations came to be. But this demarcation is not so clear in other places of the world. Consider the work of the liberation theologians of Latin America like Leonard Boff.

# Learning from "Base Communities"

Boff is a Franciscan priest who describes the "base ecclesial communities" of Brazil in his book *Ecclesiogenesis: The Base Communities Reinvent the Church.* Boff employs the language of the basic community (as described in the seminar held in Maringá, Brazil, from May 1 to 3, 1972, which examined these communities) as "a group, or complex of groups, of persons in which a primary, personal relationship of brotherly and sisterly communion obtains, and which lives the totality of the life of the church, as expressed in service, celebration, and evangelization."[29]

Boff posits that the particular church is the universal church rendered visible within the framework of a time and a place, a medium and a culture. Every "particular church" is the universal church made flesh with all the assuming "limits of place, time, culture, and human beings." He sees the particular church as the "whole mystery of salvation in Christ—the universal church—in history, but not the totality of the history of the mystery of salvation in Christ."[30] Meaning, each of these particular church communities is sacramental, a means of God's embodied grace in the world.

Being that the basic church communities represent, in part, the "true, universal church" they can revolutionize the church by turning the focus from structure to community. Boff defines *ecclesiogenesis* as "birthing the church" or "starting the church again." He argues that basic church communities help shift the hierarchical structure of the church from "steeple down" to "foundation up" by giving laity a greater level of shared power in the church.[31] Boff reminds us that Jesus "preached the kingdom of God, not the church"[32] and yet through his life, death, resurrection, and sending of the Spirit, the church was born.

---

29. 2 Ibid.

30. 3 Ibid.

31. 4 Ibid.

32. 5 Ibid., 56.

Boff describes that in the first Pentecost, "the Spirit descended upon all present and caused each one to hear the same message, albeit in a diversity of languages. It did not make all speak the same language. It made all hear the same message." The prefiguring of the "one . . . Catholic ... Church"—is a demonstration of both the oneness and catholicity of the church, with one and the same universal church being enfleshed in multiple particular churches. Boff writes, "In their own particular way, the basic ecclesial communities incarnate this experience of salvation. Therefore they are indeed authentic universal church become reality at the grassroots."[33] We have called what Boff describes here, "togetheversity" or communities whose locus of being is *doing justice together*.

Boff argues that base communities are not just another movement within the church, but rather these are churches in themselves, among the people, in the church's foundations. He writes, "The basic communities are a response to the question: How may the community's experience of the apostolic faith be embodied and structured in the conditions of a people who, in Brazil as throughout Latin America, are both religious and oppressed?"[34]

Christians who are deaf to the cry of the oppressed are not Christian at all. Churches cannot merely legitimate the dominant social and religious status quo. Boff writes that these communities have "emerged as a factor for protest and for the development of liberative ideas. This is what is occurring in the basic church communities, deeply and consistently. Here practical alternatives spring from a living evangelical experience of faith—in response to a prophetic denunciation of the abuses of the system in all its antipopular structure—with courage, but without great social resonance" . . . "Life is celebrated, the life of a faith lived in the struggles of the everyday, and the ones celebrating are the people, these people so filled with drama and tragedy."[35]

---

33. 6 Ibid.
34. 7 Ibid.
35. 8 Ibid.

The base communities recover the subversive nature of the church. They connect people into what sociologist Manuel Castells calls "resistance identity," which is generated by actors who are in devalued conditions within the dominant structures but who embody values opposed to those permeating the institutions of society. The identity of resistance leads to the formation of communes or communities, which is collective resistance against oppression or the dominant culture defined by history, geography, or biology.[36]

These small faith communities of resistance help people connect and organize at a grassroots level. They can then "refashion the social fabric and rebuild the people permanently, as agents of their own fate, coresponsible for the building of a livable communality for all."[37]

It's easy to see how these communities reintegrate church planting and social justice. Leonardo Boff zeroes in on what we've tried to articulate about "fresh expressions" and "church renewal" as essentially two ways of saying the same thing, not to be dichotomized or pitted against one another, "In other words the basic church communities, while signifying the communitarian aspect of Christianity, and signifying it within the church, cannot pretend to constitute a global alternative to the church as institution. They can only be its ferment for renewal."[38]

Boff argues that we cannot get to ecclesial renewal without ecclesiogenesis. He illustrates the dynamics of a blended ecology of church. Base communities, what we call "Fresh Expressions" bring the communitarian elements into coexistence with the institutional elements, which leads to wholistic renewal. We like to refer to this as giving birth to raise the dead.

These Fresh Expressions of Church recombine social justice and church planting in ways that have long been broken apart. We could define them as *justice-oriented expressions of church.*

---

36.  9 Manuel Castells, The Power of Identity, 2nd ed., vol. 2 of The Information Age: Economy, Society, and Culture (Malden, MA: Wiley-Blackwell, 2010), 8-9.

37.  10 Boff, 87.

38.  11 Ibid.

# Cultivating Justice-Oriented Expressions

So how do we go about creating these communities? During different periods the church has gone about mission and church planting in harmful ways. We have done mission in the name of Jesus, but not in the way of Jesus. That always causes more harm than good.

The intrinsic motivation of Jesus was not dominance and expansion, but rather, compassion. "When Jesus saw the crowds, he had compassion for them because they were troubled and helpless, like sheep without a shepherd" (Matthew 9:36).

The Greek word for compassion, *splanchnizomai*: means to be moved as to one's bowels, hence, to be moved with compassion. The bowels were thought to be the seat of love and mercy. So, Jesus has a gut-wrenching love that inspires him to act.

The unbounded mercy of God manifests in Jesus's ministry of compassion and finds ultimate expression in the cross. The church as the "body of Christ" (1 Corinthians 12:27) in the world is an expression of Christ's own compassion. An active, practical, inclusive compassion should emanate endlessly from the church.

For Christians compassion is not mere emotionality, but rather a new mode of being, empowered by the Spirit. Its embodiment requires a new and different ecclesiology that counteracts the dominate social stratification.[39] Thus, compassion-centered expressions of church will be inclusive of all, regardless of age, status, race, or gender.

We believe that Philippians 2, the "mind of Christ" provides a framework for the kind of incarnational mission that brings justice-oriented expressions into being. This is a journey that starts with self-emptying, being vulnerable, and immersing ourselves fully in a context, where we can "mind the gaps" of the fragmentation in our communities. There the compassion of Christ can be embodied through us in new and creative ways.

---

39.  12 Louw, D. J., 2016, "Missio Dei as embodiment of Passio Dei: the role of God-images in the Mission-outreach and pastoral caregiving of the church – a hermeneutical approach," Missionalia: Southern African Journal of Missiology, 44(3):336–354.

The person of Jesus, his journey of incarnation, cross, resurrection, ascension, and sending of the Spirit, is the foundation for the framework we propose. Paul implores the church community to have the "same mind . . . that was in Christ Jesus" (verse 5 NRSVUE). Then he describes it step by step:

Adopt the attitude that was in Christ Jesus:

> Though he was in the form of God,
>> he did not consider being equal with God
>> something to exploit.
>> But he emptied himself
>> by taking the form of a slave
>> and by becoming like human beings.
> When he found himself in the form of a human,
>> he humbled himself by becoming obedient
>> to the point of death,
>> even death on a cross.
> Therefore, God highly honored him
>> and gave him a name above all names,
>> so that at the name of Jesus everyone
>> in heaven, on earth, and under the earth might bow
>> and every tongue confess
>> that Jesus Christ is Lord, to the glory of God the Father.
>> (Philippians 2:5-11 CEB)

Jesus's incarnation is the "way" we should go about evangelism, discipleship, social justice, and church planting. We describe that pathway as the *passional journey*. Think of it as a pathway for your team to travel together toward creating justice-oriented expressions. This diagram describes each move highlighted in Philippians 2, correlated with a corresponding move in the passional journey:

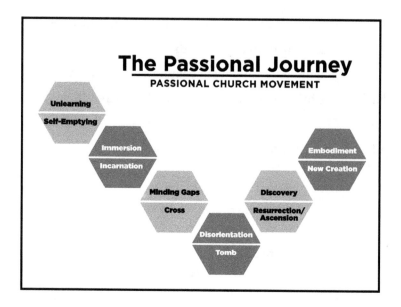

These moves could be called the *fundamentals of incarnation*—the ultimate contextualization. However, we've broken them out specifically as Paul describes them, while also filling in details from the Gospels.

For our purposes, we will simply identify each of the moves and provide the theological underpinnings.

### (1) Self-emptying (unlearning)

The first move is about humility, "emptying self." One way to understand the significance of Jesus's self-emptying is to explore his normal development as a human being. While remaining fully God, he did indeed grow in his understanding (Luke 2:41-52). Jesus grew up in Nazareth and was called a Nazarene (Matthew 2:23), and he "grew in wisdom and stature, and is favor with God and [humanity]" (Luke 2:52 NIV). Perhaps this was a kind of intentional "unlearning." The carpenter of the universe became the carpenter's son. While the mystery of the Incarnation only allows us to go so far with this idea, "fully human and fully God" is an irresolvable paradox, after all. These texts demonstrate a humility in which Jesus "empties" and goes through the normal human developmental process. The humility to empty, to unlearn, to embrace vulnerability, is a fundamental characteristic of the mind of Christ (Philippians 2:7-8).

For the church, this initial move requires, first and foremost, humility. Our mental models were formed in a world that is fading from view. We don't have all the answers, and we have asked the wrong questions. This emptying process includes some of our foundational assumptions as a primarily attractional, propositional, segregated, and colonial iteration of the church. It can include identifying racist ideas and structures now that we are aware of the invisible pyramid we inhabit.

Thus, the first move in the passional journey is unlearning: to cleanse the gates of perception; to consciously choose to give up, abandon, or stop using knowledge, values, or behaviors to acquire new ones. In the organizational sense, it includes a process of clearing out old routines and beliefs that no longer meet current challenges.[40] This enables us to see our communities again with fresh eyes.

## (2) Incarnation (immersion)

The second move is about vulnerability. Through the Incarnation, while Jesus remains sinless, he descends into a human condition that is ultimately fallen and marred. He takes a risk. The Incarnation—God coming in human flesh—is a missional endeavor. While the kingdoms of the world oppress and take captive a train of innocents in their self-seeking agendas, Jesus comes in selfless love and ultimate humiliation (crucifixion). God immerses himself fully in the context of humanity. The universal One enters into particularity. Jesus brings healing to the cosmos, not by manipulating it from the outside but through living a cruciform life in the middle of it—true contextualization.

In the North American context, Jesus's very life and death provides a model for our mission. Hence, incarnation is the form of our mission. The church as the body of Christ is an extension of the very incarnate

---

40.   13 Makoto Matsuo, "Goal Orientation, Critical Reflection, and Unlearning: An Individual-Level Study," *Human Resource Development Quarterly* 29, no. 1 (2018): 50.

flesh-and-blood Jesus that we proclaim, a channel of God's grace in the world.

Thus, immersion is the next move in the framework: the action of immersing someone or something in a context. We must immerse ourselves in our communities in risky, vulnerable ways. Through immersion, we learn about the people in our community outside the church walls. What are their fears and challenges, what are their hopes and dreams?

## (3) Cross (minding the gaps)

The third move requires a willingness to sacrifice. Jesus willingly gives his life in the most devastating and shameful way possible. Here we see echoes of the "suffering servant" passage of Isaiah 53. There is no doubt that some of Paul's references to the form of God contrasts between humanity grasping for equality with God and Jesus self-emptying. Philippians 2 mirrors Genesis 3. Humanity takes the fruit of temptation in an attempt to be like God. Jesus, who is the very form of God, empties himself and takes on the form of sin-marred humanity to redeem the fallen condition.

There is a gap between the covenant God has made with humanity and our ability to live it out. The cross is the bridge God builds across the gap. Jesus, the God-human, takes on all the forces of wickedness. On the cross, he turns human ego and violence in on itself. He himself bears our sins in his body on the cross so that, free from sins, we might live for righteousness; by his wounds we have been healed (1 Peter 2:24).

He comes down and lives out the redemptive act that transfigures eternity. N. T. Wright, reflecting on Colossians 2, insists that in the cross, the "rulers and the powers" have been defeated through the forgiveness of sins.[41] "He disarmed the rulers and authorities and made a public example of them, triumphing over them in it" (Colossians 2:15 NRSVUE). Jesus is the way God heals the gap.

---

41.    14 N. T. Wright, *The Day the Revolution Began: Reconsidering the Meaning of Jesus's Crucifixion* (San Francisco: HarperOne, 2016), 257.

Thus, the church is not in the self-preservation business; the church is in the self-donation business. The very eucharistic nature of the body of Christ is to break pieces of ourselves off and give them away to a hungry world. Unfortunately, when our church is caught in a decline cycle, we clench our fists, desperately grasping at what's left. Yet if we open our hands and give what we are away through our own self-death, we release God to catalyze resurrection (John 12:24). Infilled by the Holy Spirit, we as the church descend into the messy brokenness of those who suffer as the hands and feet of Jesus. We stand in the tragic gaps with Jesus, bringing healing and reconciliation.

Thus, this move in the framework is minding the gaps, which originates from a visual-warning phrase issued to subway riders to be careful crossing the spatial gap between the train door and the station platform. For our purposes, this is seeing the sore spots, the fragmentation, the disconnects in our community, the injustice, the institutional voids where we need to sacrificially build relational bridges. Where is this invisible pyramid causing inequity and harm, how do we begin to dismantle it together?

## (4) Tomb (disorientation)

The fourth move requires faith and obedience in the face of uncertainty. An often-overlooked component of the Incarnation is the three days that Jesus spends in the grave. God doesn't stop where we live but goes before us into death. Meeting with us in our brokenness, Jesus does not bail out when things get uncomfortable; he willingly gives his life. He trusts the Father and moves into the unknown.

Yet Romans 6:4 and Colossians 2:12 reveal not only the astonishing depths of God's love but also our place with him in the tomb. This descent into the tomb with Christ is part of our own journey to spiritual maturity. It is a move toward our own resurrection life. This inverts the modern world's values of honor, prestige, and power.

The tomb forces us into an uncomfortable state of liminality and confusion. We join the disoriented march back to our familiar Emmaus, saying, "But we had hoped that he was the one to redeem Israel. Yes, and besides all this, it is now the third day since these things took place" (Luke 24:21 NRSVUE).

The tomb represents separation, disorientation, and living in the in-between. As we carry the cross, innovate, and create new things, we hit the wall of disappointment and failure. Challenging a system of racialization that stretches back centuries is not easy or quick work. It can feel like taking apart a pyramid one stone at a time. We will fail. There will be pushback. Sometimes people in our own inner circle will abandon or sabotage the work. It's in those very moments when we are completely dependent upon the Holy Spirit that we must press through, one moment, one hour, one day at a time.

Thus, in the framework, disorientation describes the state of having lost one's sense of direction and meaning. Organizationally speaking, this is living on the edge of chaos, between stagnation and innovation.[42]

## (5) Resurrection/ascension (discovery)

The fifth move is about God's supernatural intervention and how that epiphany opens our awareness to the possibility of resurrection life. In the Resurrection, we discover the victory of God over sin, shame, and suffering. We see the image of the invisible God once hidden and the deep mystery now revealed that in the Christ even the Gentiles have been saved (Colossians 1:24-29), something veiled since the foundation of the world (Ephesians 3:1-13). It's the final fulfillment of the Abrahamic Promise where we started. It is in confessing Jesus as Lord and believing God raised him from the dead, through which we are saved (Romans 10:9).

The first Christians experienced Jesus, through the power of the Holy Spirit, as infinitely alive on both personal and communal levels (1

---

42.   15 Michael Moynagh, Church in Life: Innovation, Mission, and Ecclesiology (Eugene, OR: Cascade, 2018), 34.

Corinthians 12:3). It is the discovery of Christ's victory in the Resurrection that humanity finds restoration from its fragmented condition. Jesus has ultimately bridged the gap as the still incarnate and risen Christ.

It wasn't until the Resurrection that the disciples were transformed in their perceptions, resulting in a new mental model. In the language of Alcoholics Anonymous, they experienced an entire psychic change. This transformation is captured by the biblical concept of Μετανοέω: to change one's mind, to turn in another direction, a transformative change of heart, especially a spiritual conversion (eventually translated as "repent"). Metanoia literally means "afterthought," from meta, meaning "after" or "beyond," and nous, meaning "mind."

Resurrection = Discovery = metanoeō

Think of the transformation that takes place in the disciples after they encounter the risen Jesus. Mary hears him speak her name and moves from mourning to celebratory worship (John 20:16). Their "eyes were opened" to who he was in the breaking of the bread (Luke 24:31); Peter was reinstated after denial (John 21:15-17); Thomas proclaimed, "My Lord and my God!" after being invited to touch the wounds (John 20:24-29); and so on. Their concepts of the Messiah, from conquering king to crucified and now risen Lord went through a metamorphosis based on the discovery of the Resurrection. Up until Jesus's arrest and even beyond to the reports of the empty tomb, they continued to misunderstand who he was. In his resurrected body, he opens the Scriptures to them (Luke 24:27) and gifts them with the Holy Spirit (John 20:19-23). Through these encounters, they become entirely different people.

Peter Senge defines metanoia as simply "real learning," the kind that gets to the heart of being human.[43] This is a radical shift in awareness, the fundamental shift of mind. The kingdom of God is at hand, but you need a shift of mind to see it. He goes on to say that "learning is leading."

---

43. 16 Senge, Peter, The Fifth Discipline: The Art & Practice of the Learning Organization (New York: Doubleday, 2006), 13-14.

Metanoia is an unending process of unlearning, learning, and relearning. We need shifts in our ecological, social, political, economic, emotional, relational, and spiritual understanding. It doesn't happen by merely reading books or downloading new data, we have to bring our heart and hands to the work. This kind of transformation comes through bringing our bodies together with other bodies as we form new creation communities. There we discover the risen Jesus, liberator of the oppressed, in our midst. Discovery transitions us into knowing what to do.

Thus, in the framework, this move is described as discovery, the action or process of attaining new insight. New discoveries lead to innovation. Once we move through the process of liminality and disorientation, our reality can be transformed. However, if the discovery is not scaled or downloaded and spread throughout the system, it fails. This leads us to the final move: embodiment.

## (6) New Creation (embodiment):

The final move is about a new form of embodiment, ranging from a transformed habitus individually to the formation of a new communal manifestation of Jesus's life. Meaning, taking this journey may lead to a new you, a new ministry, a new contextual Christian community, and so on. Philippians 2 envisions an ascended Lord, surrounded by a new communal embodiment consisting of every knee and every tongue bent and confessing "in heaven, on earth, and under the earth," heralding a transformation that is cosmic in scope. Philippians 3:17–4:1 envisions the mature community living a resurrected life now with our citizenship already in heaven.

Ephesians 4 further informs the meaning of the Ascension for this new colony of heaven on earth. The resurrected body of Jesus on the throne is not the only body. Jesus has a body on the earth as well—the church. The church is filled and gifted by the Spirit. Jesus, the head of the church, has given us the mind of Christ. He who fills all things (Ephesians 4:10) and who has poured out his Spirit on all people (Acts 2:14-21) is bringing the healing of the cosmos (Romans 8:19-23).

For better or worse, the gifts God gives to the church is us—gifted persons (Ephesians 4:10-11). An embodied and gifted community called the church is God's missional instrument of reconciliation on the earth.

Thus, the final move of the framework is described as embodiment, the tangible or visible form of an idea, quality, or, in our case, a person. The mind of Christ is now embodied in a community.

# The Blended Ecology: Joining God's Diversity

The passional journey is an approach to mission in the way of Jesus. We offer it as a framework to think about cultivating justice-oriented expressions of church. These fresh expressions are forms of church that get us back to a Luke 10 kind of blueprint. Built into the process are elements of social justice, as we "mind the gaps" and love and serve the people in our community, building relationships with them over time.

This prayerful journey of cultivating new Christian communities throughout a parish or region, includes an innate motivation to join God's diversity often already in the larger community (Luke 10).

These new forms of Christian community take shape through building relationships with the diverse people of the larger community. In that sense, they are an embodiment of justice, in that they seek reconciliation and wholistic relationships rather than preserving the status quo of segregation. Implicit in these relationships is shared power dynamics. Unlike other harmful mission approaches across the span of history, there is a built-in mutuality. Partners enter these relationships as equals. Loving and serving is not about providing handouts, it's about people self-organizing, harnessing the intrinsic motivation to build a better community together.

In the process of this, Christians naturally share their faith in the context of abiding relationships. Not in an attempt to snatch people back to the compound for Christianization, but in the shared commitment to heal a community. People of various faiths and no-faith can work together through shared empowerment. These communities make one aspect of their life a commitment to social justice. They are aimed at real flesh-and-blood needs and wants. They see and work to alleviate suffering and inequality. Relationships are strengthened as we love and serve together.

This model of action and leadership puts the focus back where it belongs: on the whole people of God. Your community is suffering? What are you going to do together to make a difference? No one gets to be a pew warmer in this game; everyone is sent out in teams.

These emerging base ecclesial communities, or fresh expressions, live in a blended ecology with inherited congregations. It's not abandoning the more traditional forms of church, it's about multiple forms living together in a symbiotic relationship. Over time, the smaller and more experimental forms of church begin to have an impact on the inherited congregation. The diversity seemingly spills back into the cracks in the stained glass. The culture of the existing congregations is transformed as they live in relationship with justice-oriented expressions. In our experience, this is a powerful way to heal racialization within inherited systems. Which leads us to our final move . . . reorganizing structures.

## The Next Step

- The previous chapter suggested that the omission of the word "Go" in The United Methodist mission statement creates a scenario in which all the arrows are pointing inward toward the church, whereas Jesus sends the disciples out into the world. Jesus teaches his disciples to be guests, dependent on the hospitality of others (Lk 10:1-9). The church in the US has largely played host in an attractional only paradigm... "you come to us at a place we have decided, at a time we have set, in a manner we have determined." As you reflect on the life and ministries of your congregation, draw a diagram of your church building using a whiteboard or stick-up paper. Do an audit of the ministries of your church. For each ministry, group, or worship service, designate an arrow either pointing inward or outward. How many ministries in your church send disciples out into the world to be the church, rather than inviting outsiders to the church?

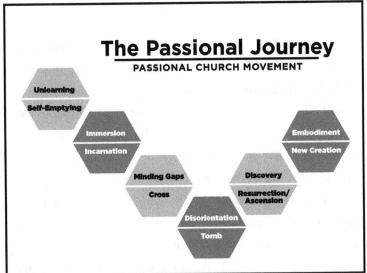

- Review the passional journey together. Let the following questions guide your conversation:
- What preconceptions do we need to shed? What do we need to unlearn?

- What are we noticing as we immerse ourselves in the community?

- Where are there gaps between the fullness of the kingdom of God and what we are seeing and sensing in our community?

- Where is God already at work?

- What are signs of the kingdom of God already here?

- What might embodiment of the good news of God's kingdom look like/feel like/sound like/taste like here?

- How must we change in response to what we're learning about our parish?

## "Finally Seen"

*Pastor Raimon 'Rai' Jackson*
*The Well, Washington D.C.*

The story of healing and hope for the community of The Well, based out of the metropolitan area of Maryland and Washington D.C., is initiated daily by our approach to intense and often uncomfortable conversations of taboo. The Well is a creative arts and conscious awareness faith community. It's an expression of the church that unites community, embraces the arts, navigates purpose, and evokes healthy conversation around spirituality, justice, and Jesus.

It all begins with the unapologetic audacity to ask the tough questions from multiple perspectives while allowing the space for complete and honest dialogue even when it causes unease. Providing the space for a far right conservative black male to engage with a far left liberal white male, or asking a gentrifier what it feels like to be a part of the system, or calling out the blasphemed models of a white Jesus and the harmful effects of a heavily influenced Eurocentric Christianity that has perpetuated the undertones of a racist American culture, are just some of the conversations we have initiated on our platform.

The Well not only wrestles with the behavior and actions of racism, but we also focus on healing from an introspective cultural lens. It is necessary to detangle many of the stigmas that too often are a thread between minority societies to issues such as lack of self-confidence and even internal discrimination. Hosting platforms such as "Is the black church still relevant?" and "Who in the black church matters," where we seek to unpack generational gaps within the black culture as well as gender representation and human sexuality within the context of the black culture. We find hope in providing the atmosphere for education and representation.

Perhaps the best way to explain the efforts of The Well's platform as it relates to racism is to share some of the responses expressed from and to our community. One participant exclaims joyously, "I finally felt seen." This was a young man's response to being invited to and accepted on a Christian platform despite his identity as a young black member of the LGBTQ community. Others have stated "Wow! If only we could experience love like this on the daily." This comment has been conveyed many different times from both guests and participants in the chat. Our rules demand respect for those who agree and disagree with each other. It requires that you truly listen and respond with love regardless of perspective. We reiterate that we are not focused on changing anyone's mind on any particular subject, but rather we focus on the humanity, the spirituality and the opportunity to love one another as we are woven together as a spiritual family all created in the Imago Dei.

The Well aspires to serve as a beacon of connectedness and a symbol of true love in the plight for equity and equality. Just as the woman at the well encountered Jesus and her life was changed because of his willingness to converse with her in spite of her dispositions, her ways, and the traditions of that time, we, too, believe that our Well Encounters offer a very similar experience for all who partake in healthy dialogue with each other. We seize the opportunity to not just have church, but to be the church. A family that, despite our differences, can recognize our connectedness through the same source, God.

# Reflection

What strikes you about Rai's story about The Well community? What actions can you take to create an environment that allows for these kinds of conversations? What would healing racialization look like if this story took place in your congregation?

# CHAPTER 5

# Reorganizing Structures

*They will rebuild ancient ruins on your account;*
*the foundations of generations past you will restore.*
*You will be called Mender of Broken Walls,*
*Restorer of Livable Streets.*
*(Isaiah 58:12 CEB)*

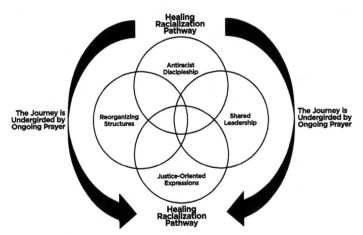

The structures of society, organizations, and even the church perpetuate racialization. When structures are forged from the alloy of racism, militarism, and materialism, they need to be dismantled, melted down, purified, and reorganized. We will never have a more just and equitable world until we deal with this reality.

All we have shared so far fails if we don't include this fourth circle in the healing racialization pathway. As Ibram Kendi reminds us, it is not racist ideas that create racist policies, but rather it is these racist structures and policies that create, perpetuate, and enforce racist ideas.[44] It's not that if we change our minds, we will be able to overcome racism; we need to change policy. It's not racist people that perpetuate racism, it's racist structures that make racist people. This final move is the actual work of dismantling the invisible pyramid.

This work involves changing legislation and policies. You might assume those are the tasks of politicians and lawmakers only, but this leads to another faulty mindset that's prevalent in the church: the separation of politics and religion.

You've heard the old cliché, any topic is up for discussion at family gatherings, except for politics and religion. Nothing seems to stir controversy like those two words. But, as Christians, let's return to the life and teachings of Jesus, and take our instruction from him.

Jesus's central proclamation focused on the "kingdom of God." In his life and ministry, that kingdom was breaking into the kingdoms of the world in a fresh way. He proclaimed an alternative kingdom and claimed to be its long-awaited messiah-king. He demanded justice for the oppressed and marginalized and called to account the powers and principalities. These actions and ideas were of the kingdom of God. And they were politically subversive acts amidst the subjugation of the Roman Empire.

The nature of Jesus's invitation to repent and enter the kingdom was and is entirely *political.*

# Let's Get Political

Greater than our identification as a Democrat or a Republican, is our identity as a *Christian.* That is our fundamental "political position," and being a follower of Jesus is a deeply political endeavor. The two-party system of US imperialism is secondary to the kingdom that Jesus proclaimed. Disciples of Jesus are to be in the world but not of it (John 17:14-18). For thousands of years Christians have spoken out about the evils of various

---

44. Kendi, Ibram X. *How to be an Antiracist,* 44.

governments and societal structures and have been marginalized, exiled, and even executed for doing so.

Jesus is known as Savior, King, and Lord. He has claimed dominion over his followers' lives and our political allegiance is to him alone. The values we seek to embody, albeit imperfectly, are taken from his own life and teaching. We communicate, report to, and submit to his rule afresh each day. Jesus's Sermon on the Mount (Matthew 5–7) is the political manifesto we seek to live by.

Jesus regularly called out the evil of the religious leadership of his day (Matthew 12:4; John 8:44; Matthew 23:27) and the appointed politicians (Luke 13:32), while proclaiming a new political system was breaking into the world called the "kingdom of God," which was embodied in himself (Mark 1:14-15). The Gospels appropriated the common language of the Roman political system "κύριος" ("Lord" used as a title for the Caesars), "εὐαγγέλιον" ("gospel" used to describe the "good news" of the Pax Romana of Caesar Augustus), . . . "βασιλείας" (kingdom), and "υἱὸς θεός" ("Son of God" also used to describe the divine-human nature of the Caesars).

Jesus was tried and executed by the convergence of a bankrupt religious system and the imperial power of Rome. Jesus' execution was very political . . .

> The Jewish leaders cried out, "Take him away! Take him away! Crucify him!"
> Pilate responded, "What? Do you want me to crucify your king?"
> "We have no king except the emperor," the chief priests answered. Then Pilate handed Jesus over to be crucified. (John 19:15-16 CEB)

It was the trumped-up charges of sedition, blasphemy, and claims connected to a messianic kingdom that landed Jesus on the cross.

Furthermore, there is an entire prophetic tradition throughout the Old Testament, ending in the Book of Revelation, of servants of God "getting political" confronting the corruption of kings, priests, and empires.

Perhaps then it should seem peculiar when we hear statements like, "Pastors should not get political" or "Leave politics out of the church"?

# The Myth of Christian Nations

Part of the issue in the US is our assumption that we are a "Christian nation." In a sense, the US church is in the middle of an identity crisis. We suffer from a kind of missional amnesia, in which a fundamental aspect of our identity has been lost. This problem has a deep history. The North American version of Christianity that most of us inherited goes back to Emperor Constantine in AD 313. Up until Constantine, Christians were a rogue, and periodically illegal, religious movement that experienced several rounds of imperial persecution. At times, the primitive church met in secret spaces, scratching the fish symbol (*Ichthys*) on cave walls to identify meeting places.

This small renegade movement, with no buildings, no professional clergy, no committee meetings, between the time of Jesus's death on the cross in the 30s and Constantine in the 300s, grew numerically across vast geographical distances. With no program of evangelism, no formal mission statements, and few resources, they became a force to be reckoned with.

While the growth of the church up until that point is difficult to explain, the explosion of growth after AD 312 is quite explainable. Emperor Constantine with his vision of a cross and voice from the sky saying, "in this sign conquer," changed the course of history and the identity of the church forever. Constantine had a history of self-aggrandizing visions, and military conquests that sealed his power. Perhaps the emperor was operating more out of a political necessity than spiritual conversion—he was not actually baptized until he lay on his deathbed twenty-five years later in AD 337. Regardless, he transformed the faith like few individuals in history.

Emperor Constantine's adoption of Christianity as the state religion was a brilliant political maneuver. This birthed the Constantinian system that continues into our inherited US version of the church. Initially this adoption had an incredible and powerfully relieving effect for those early Christians. First, they no longer had to fear being arrested or killed for following Christ. Secondly, confiscated properties were eventually returned.

The blending of religion and state power also had negative effects. The church devolved at times into a hotbed of scandal, gross extravagance, and hypocrisy. The professional clergy model was born, and, in a sense, Jesus was dethroned, replaced by the emperor. Vast church building projects were launched of unparalleled grandeur in human history.

In 1517, Martin Luther produced his 95 Theses (legend has it he nailed them to the door of the Wittenberg Castle Church). Inadvertently these troublesome formulations began the fragmentation process that resulted in the multitude of competing mini-Christendoms of denominations today.

Of course, while the Christendom church has many blemishes, she also has many beauty marks. Much of the hypercritical stereotypes of emerging generations fail to take into consideration how the church has transformed the world for the better. The church has gifted the world with hospitals, universities, shelters, and food banks. Not to mention the movements like abolition, women's suffrage, civil rights, and so on, each largely pioneered by Christian leaders. Christians have served as the moral leaven in ancient and modern times, lifting the gaze of humanity to the higher virtues.

Yet the version of Christianity we have inherited in the US is not the fish-scratching, secret-meeting-in-caves version. It is primarily an *attractional only* model: *build it and they will come.* Overseen by professional clergy, who receive special tax exceptions from the empire. It operates in the Christendom assumptions that we are a Christian nation and most of the people are already Christian. There is expectation in this arrangement that good people will go to church, as it is a cultural norm. The empire and the church work together as complementing institutions that shape the behavior and societal norms. Gregory Boyd calls this "The myth of America as a Christian nation."[45]

---

45. Gregory A. Boyd, *The Myth of a Christian Nation : How the Quest for Political Power Is Destroying the Church* (Grand Rapids, MI: Zondervan, 2005), 13.

When we study closely the life of Jesus, we can see that his church and US imperialism actually make strange bedfellows.

# Fish Bowl: The Water We Breathe

Over the past many decades in the US, the "pastor" has been seen as a kind of spiritual butler or chaplain to the imperial church. We have knowingly and sometimes unwittingly given safe harbor to racism, sexism, nationalism, and consumerism in our congregations. We and our churches have turned a blind eye while harm was being done, which is equivalent to doing the harm ourselves. We have glimpsed opportunities to do good, to speak out, to exhort and proclaim for justice, but we have allowed the opportunities to pass. And today we see a multitude of people who claim to be Christians supporting politicians who claim to be Christians, even though their actions and words are blatantly un-Christian.

But this bleak view of pastors doesn't describe all of us, maybe not even most of us. Many of us are called to reach the emerging generations who have seen these incongruencies and rejected the church outright. Successive generations seem to be questioning the amalgamation of Christ and empire. Many of us pastors—maybe you?—are trying to reclaim the early church, by reaching forward into the kingdom of God breaking in from the future.

As clergypersons, we're taking responsibility for our role, repenting, and seeking the renewal of the church. This includes naming and confronting evil.

One reason so few pastors actually "get political" in the public square or from the pulpit is that it would cost them members and money. This is a tool of the enemy to render the church silent and ineffective. The church cannot shy away from the reality of these clashing kingdoms. We are not called to be peacekeepers; we are called to be "peacemakers" (Matthew 5:9 NRSVUE). We should seek to be involved in the political process in ways that bring equality and peace.

As Gutiérrez notes, this political participation is nothing new. In the Global South clergy have always participated directly in political life, and increasingly so since the genesis of liberation theology. "The new dimension is that many priests clearly admit the need and obligation to make such a commitment and above all that their options in one way or another place them in a relationship of subversion regarding the existing social order."[46] Clergy are finding renewed meaning for the priesthood in their commitment to the oppressed and the struggle for liberation.

## Shepherds Who Don't Run

I (Michael) can remember visiting the martyrdom site of Father Stanley Rother (March 27, 1935 – July 28, 1981) at Santiago Atitlán, in Guatemala. The blood spatter from his execution is preserved under plexiglass on the wall where he was murdered. Rother was an American Roman Catholic priest from Oklahoma, and the first US-born priest and martyr to be beatified by the Catholic Church. He was murdered in Guatemala in 1981 after working there as a missionary priest since 1968.

In her book, *The Shepherd Who Didn't Run: Blessed Stanley Rother, Martyr from Oklahoma*, María Ruiz Scaperlanda documents the course of events that led to his martyrdom at the young age of 46. Multiple sources corroborate that Rother's ministry of education, farming techniques, and a radio broadcast in Spanish and the indigenous Tz'utujil language was perceived as a threat to some governmental leaders of Guatemala.

Scaperlanda posits that it was to the government's advantage that the poor remain poor and that the uneducated remain uneducated. In this way, Father Rother's ministry was subversive to the status quo. As opposition organized and grew, catechists and parishioners would disappear and later be found dead, their corpses showing signs of beating and torture. Denunciations of what the church was doing became vocal and public.

---

46. Gutiérrez, Gustavo, *A Theology of Liberation: History, Politics, and Salvation* (Maryknoll, NY: Orbis Books, 1988), 118-119.

The radio station was destroyed and its director murdered. After a brief visit to the states, Rother returned, fully aware his name was eighth on a hit list of right-wing death squads. He died standing against injustice.[47]

Standing in that holy place, seeing the bullet holes in the floor and wall where his execution took place in the church, touched me in a profound way. It shaped my own posture as a minister.

For many in the US/American context, this kind of scenario is unthinkable. Yet it highlights the radical disconnect between a clergyperson willing to oppose a government to the point of death, and our own unwillingness to "get political" because it might cost us butts and bucks. In some ways, this faulty assumption has silenced the prophetic voice of the church and shackled us in impotency and irrelevancy.

Here we want to emphasize that we are high on Jesus, low on bipartisan politics. Bipartisanship is a political situation, usually in the context of a two-party system (especially prevalent in the West), in which opposing political parties are supposed to work together to find common ground through compromise. That is the theory. What this usually looks like is two opposing parties fighting against each other to protect their own self-interests and power. In the midst of that temporal reality, to proclaim Jesus is Lord is to place our allegiance with another kingdom and another kind of political system. It is in some ways a rejection of the two opposing options. That is a deeply political place to stand!

When it comes to reorganizing structures, we think it's dangerous to closely align ourselves with one political party or the other. Both hold value, and both are deeply flawed. We can see that Jesus encountered a similar political milieu in the first century, and his unwillingness to take a side certainly contributed to his public execution (John 18:36). We cannot assume as our own the political principles of either the Republican or Democratic parties. We have been given a different set of principles, revealed in the scriptures, which reach their climax in the Sermon on the

47. Scaperlanda, María Ruiz, *The Shepherd Who Didn't Run: Blessed Stanley Rother, Martyr from Oklahoma*, revised edition (Huntington, IN: Our Sunday Visitor Publishing Division, Our Sunday Visitor, Inc, 2019).

Mount. The church has a unique politic and body of ethics all her own, and this is a gift to the world.

Therefore, we cannot use the tactics of other political systems. Ours is centered in and sustained by the life, death, resurrection, and fully alive now Jesus. His tactics are to be our own. A way of nonviolent resistance, that seeks to build a community that embodies the way of his kingdom now. This sounds great in theory, simple, right? It is simple, but not easy. The political systems in which we live seems so broken and all consuming. It's easy to assume those kingdoms are real, and the kingdom of Jesus is an unattainable ideal in this life. We need shepherds who don't run but who face these realities.

Is there a recent model of where this might work in the world? We think so.

## Unlikely Friendships: A Black Baptist, Brown Hindu, and White Evangelist

So, a Black Baptist civil rights activist, a Brown devout Hindu, and a White Methodist evangelist . . . walk into a bar. This is not a corny joke, it describes the unlikely friendship of E. Stanley Jones and Mahatma Gandhi, "the great-souled one," and the impact their relationship would one day have on Martin Luther King, Jr.

Gandhi is known for his nonviolent philosophy of passive resistance, which transformed the entire nation of India. Gandhi started his activism as an Indian immigrant in South Africa in the early 1900s. After World War I, he became the leading figure in India's struggle to gain independence from Great Britain. He was imprisoned several times during his pursuit of non-cooperation, led multiple mass fasts, and undertook a number of hunger strikes to protest the injustice and oppression of India's poorest classes.

The self-governing independent India and Pakistan legally came into existence at midnight on 14-15 August 1947. The Partition of British

India in 1947 refers to the change of political borders and the division of other assets that accompanied the dissolution of the British Raj in South Asia and the creation of two independent dominions: India and Pakistan. After the Partition, Gandhi continued to work toward peace between Hindus and Muslims. He was assassinated by a Hindu fundamentalist in Delhi on January 30, 1948.

Gandhi's life and movement attracted the attention of a young Methodist missionary to India named E. Stanley Jones (1884–1973). Jones was also a theologian, evangelist, and author born in Baltimore, Maryland, who also served on the faculty of Asbury College in Wilmore, Kentucky. He was called to missionary service in India in 1907 and began working with the lowest castes, including Dalits. Jones was the architect of a series of interreligious lectures (or "round tables") to the educated classes in India. Thousands of these lectures were held across the Indian subcontinent during the first decades of the twentieth century. One of his most well-known books was *The Christ of the Indian Road*, which sold more than a million copies worldwide in 1925.

In addition to the round table conferences, Jones felt the need for a spiritual base. He envisioned a retreat for spiritual refreshment, where there could be in-depth study and reflection in the company of a close-knit group. Thus, he began a movement of Christian Ashrams (or forest retreats). *Ashram* originates from the Sanskrit word *āśrama*. An ashram would traditionally be located far from human habitation, in forests or mountainous regions, amidst refreshing natural surroundings conducive to spiritual instruction and meditation. It is a place where one strives toward a goal in a disciplined manner, which could include ascetic, spiritual, and yogic.

Jones believed that these gatherings should be in a familiar Indian context. He was convinced that the Christian faith was universal but needed to find embodiment through indigenous forms. Jones used the term *Ashram* to express this group fellowship; but he Christianized the concept with Jesus Christ as the teacher. Jones was a pioneer in the concept

**80**

of *indigenization* or making the gospel understood in the language and thought forms of the local people. His efforts included making the church more autonomous in its organization. In 1962, he was nominated for the Nobel Peace Prize for his missionary work in India and in 1963 he received the Gandhi Peace Award.

Jones befriended many leaders in the Indian Independence movement and became known for his interfaith work. Jones interpreted reconciliation as "God's chief business," that is, between God and humanity, within our own inner life, and between human beings one to another. If it is God's primary focus, it should be ours as well.[48]

Dr. Jones became a close friend of Mahatma Gandhi, the two met together in person and corresponded through letters. Gandhi challenged Jones about the Western forms of Christianity and the need for greater respect of the strengths of Indian culture and character. Gandhi's own "impossible dream" for a nonviolent revolution was inspired by Jesus's Sermon on the Mount. Gandhi helped Jones see that the love, compassion, and forgiveness embodied by Jesus was often not present in his followers. Through his relationship with Gandhi, his own missionary understanding and practice was refined.

Jones was so impacted by Gandhi that after his assassination he wrote a biography on his life. In *Gandhi: Portrayal of a Friend*, Jones argued that while not a Christian, Gandhi lived the way of Jesus. His nonviolent revolution, "demonstrated . . . on a colossal scale [that Jesus's way of love] is no longer idealism; it is stark realism. It has been demonstrated as clearly as a problem in geometry. It is pure science."[49]

Regarding Gandhi's great contribution to the world, Jones wrote, "Mahatma is God's appeal to this age—an age drifting again to its doom. If the atomic bomb was militarism's trump card thrown down on the table of human events, then Mahatma Gandhi is God's trump card which

---

48. "E. Stanley Jones," https://readthespirit.com/interfaith-peacemakers/e-stanley-jones/, accessed November 27, 2023.

49. Jones, E. Stanley. *Gandhi: Portrait of a Friend* (Nashville: Abingdon Press, 2019).

he throws down on the table of events now—a table trembling with destiny. God has to play his hand skillfully, for man is free, so God cannot coerce."[50]

Jones concluded, "I would like my readers to see the man I see . . . a little man, who fought a system in the framework of which I stand, has taught me more of the Spirit of Christ than perhaps any other man in East or West. This book is a symbol of my gratitude. . . ."[51] While the book did not receive the acclaim or recognition of *Christ of the Indian Road*, it perhaps had more transformative impact than any other of Jones's books.

For it was Jones's book on Gandhi that found its way into the possession of a young black pastor born in Atlanta, Georgia, named Martin Luther King, Jr. (January 15, 1929 – April 4, 1968). As a young pastor, King's strategic planning of the 1955 Montgomery bus boycott quickly thrust him onto the nation's stage as a leader in the US civil rights movement. Many are familiar with King's philosophy of nonviolent direct action to liberate oppressed blacks suffering in the 1950s under a system of legal segregation in the southern US. King's approach was derived from Jesus's teaching in the Sermon on the Mount (Matthew 5–7), but it was from the Hindu activist Mahatma Gandhi that King drew the methodology for putting Jesus's teachings into practice in the segregationist South. King's connection with Gandhi's life began when he first read E. Stanley Jones's biography on Gandhi.

King said, "Christ furnished the spirit and motivation, while Gandhi furnished the method." In 1959 King traveled to India to dialogue with the Gandhi family and others active in the movement to deepen his own understanding of nonviolence. Later, King told Jones's daughter, Eunice Jones Mathews, that it was this biography that inspired him to "non-violence" in the Civil Rights Movement.[52]

---

50. Ibid.

51. Ibid.

52. "How Gandhi Inspired Methodist Peacemakers," https://umcmission.org/may-2020/how-gandhi-inspired-methodist-peacemakers/, accessed November 28, 2023.

# Love Force

When it comes to reorganizing structures, there is much to learn from these three giants of the faith. The Jesus way of reorganizing structures ultimately enables us to embody what Gandhi called Satyagraha, which can mean "soul force," "truth force," and "love force." It enables us to respond to hate with love and accept hardships as the pathway to peace. Thus, it may lead us to take up justice-oriented actions like nonviolent resistance, public witness, volunteering, or working to change harmful policies and legislation. We as a community of wounded healers give ourselves to change the structures that enable and perpetuate the wicked problems that plague society.

One way to reorganize structures is through legislation that changes racist policies. This could include putting pressure on the government to tighten gun laws, lobbying to channel resources to underdeveloped neighborhoods from the result of redlining, and being involved in writing new legislation for prison reform. It could occur at an organizational level like the work of the Antiracism Task Force in Florida, in which the group brings awareness to the racial inequity and then acts to change the structures that sustain that inequality, and provides accountability when goals aren't met.

The church doesn't necessarily need to be the founder of these behaviors, in fact, it's more effective if we can join together with grassroots organizers to support their work. In most communities, there are groups of people aiming at changing legislation and policy. How can we come alongside them, resource them, and be involved in their work? Sometimes the church will need to create an initiative or task force, but this should always be done in conversation and relationship with the stakeholders who it will affect. The most infective activities of the church are born from an attitude that we have all the resources and knowledge and we need to go and fix what's broken in the community. These efforts can actually do more harm than good if we don't do it in the spirit of humility and collaboration.

In some cases, this will require us to get involved in and even co-organize peaceful protests. When injustice occurs, the church is called to be first responders to the tragedy, not the last on the scene. Organizations that align with the spiritual power of Satyagraha could be partners in the work of reorganizing structures. For example, many churches found an ally in the Black Lives Matter movement. Some would say this is a movement doing work the church should have been doing all along.

A final tool of the church, one utilized with incredible effect by Mahatma Gandhi is the mass fast. When a policy or crime of inequality becomes so unbearable that it can no longer be tolerated, people organize and literally put their lives on the line to see it change. Hunger strikes have been used effectively across history up until today. When people are willing to starve to death in order to change unjust structures it puts pressure on the government to respond in an accelerated manner. Gandhi was able to draw the attention of the available media to his fasts in such a way that aroused a global outcry. King followed suit, using the media to bring people face to face with the horrors of racism and segregation.

Jemar Tisby, in his bestselling book *How to Fight Racism: Courageous Christianity and the Journey Toward Racial Justice*, suggests several racial justice practices. Having your team budget time for racial justice—actually deciding a percentage of time and staying accountable. Giving financially to support the work as part of a tithe toward racial justice. Stop referencing, platforming, and supporting known racists across history. Use your platform, no matter how big or small, to take a stance against racism. Support minority owned businesses and organizations. Vote for political candidates committed to racial justice, or like me (Stephanie), run for office yourself! Evaluate local school systems and do a racism audit.[53]

These practices can be essential activities in your justice-oriented expressions. Activate the community to pick one or several of these practices as a part of your normal rhythm of life. You could create a "rule of life" that

---

53. Tisby, Jemar, *How to Fight Racism: Courageous Christianity and the Journey toward Racial Justice* (Grand Rapids, MI: Zondervan Reflective, 2021), 93-115.

ensures following practices aimed at reorganizing structures is an expectation of belonging to the group. Invite others who are actively engaged in seeking racial justice to come and share what they are up to. Discern ways you might support or collaborate in their work. These are just a few ways you can be about dismantling the invisible pyramid that might lead to the healing of racialization in people, communities, and organizations.

It's our prayer that God would raise up a generation of leaders who faithfully follow Jesus and have the courage to "get political." Communities who speak and embody the truth no matter what the cost. The world needs a church that is more Christian than American, and sometimes those identities present colliding values. In this time of massive reset, may that church arise again. When we seek to heal racialization, the kingdom of God breaks into the world, and we can pray with Jesus, "on earth as it is in heaven."

It is then we can be a church that embodies togetheversity. A beloved community—doing justice together.

## The Next Step

- Does your congregation actively confront racism through the preaching and teaching ministries of the church? Could a sermon series based on *Doing Justice Together* be helpful?

- As you think about the features of racism in your own community, how can you trace back racist thinking and actions to laws and policies? For example, redlining certain neighborhoods, over policing and brutality towards persons of color, inequitable sentencing and incarceration, unequal access to jobs and quality education. How might your congregation join other grassroots movements to seek to change legislation that perpetuates racism?

- Do a budget of where your church spends time. For example, how many hours a week are dedicated to planning worship, leading Bible studies, and committee meetings.

How many hours are dedicated to racial justice? Make a commitment to spend a percentage of your time on reorganizing structures. How will you be accountable as a team to this commitment?

- Decide a portion of the tithe that will be dedicated towards racial justice. What organization, grassroots movements, or activists might your team support in their work?

- Does your church tradition regularly reference, platform, and support the work of known racists across history? How might you repent of this, publicly denounce known racists, and commit to stop supporting their work?

- Name some ways you could use your congregational and personal platforms to take a stance against racism. What would a social media campaign look like towards this end? What resources will you make available to the congregation to support the work?

- Can you identify minority owned businesses and organizations in your community? How might your congregation intentionally support them?

- During election season hold informational gatherings about politicians. Do any of the candidates have a history of racism and/or supporting racist policies? Mobilize the community to vote for candidates who support dismantling racist policies. Hold these politicians accountable for their commitments.

- Are the local school systems in your community equitable for persons of color? Do a racism audit. What is the ranking of the schools? What are the racial percentages? Are teachers and staff equitably compensated? What percentage of the school is on free or reduced lunch? Meet with principals and teachers to discover what their greatest challenges are and if the church can support them in any way.

# "We Don't Have to Wait Till Heaven"

*Rev. Woojin Kang*
*At The Table, Lawrenceville, Georgia*

This story of hope started to unravel at 5 p.m. on February 5, 2023, at the launch of At The Table, a campus of The Nett Church in historic Norcross, Georgia. There, in the dim, candlelit sanctuary, stood more than fifty individuals, mostly between the ages of 20-40 representing over eight nations, cultures, tongues, and stories joining together to encounter God in a new way. As a campus of The Nett Church, At The Table stands by the NETT acronym of Nations Experiencing Transformation Together. This launch service, this fresh beginning, was a manifestation of those very words.

At The Table started following the COVID-19 pandemic, a tragic time in the US that brought forth hate, racial tension, and violence to new heights. During a prayer vigil in response to a mass shooting, a young adult wailed in tearful agony, "Honestly, right now, I hate White people." This was her honest, unfiltered heart; these words came from deep hurt. Hate being responded to with hate. Though these words were explicit, these words were a projection of unbearable pain. Knowing that there are young people like her who are hurting, who are forming resentment toward others, what could a church do? How could church be a place of healing, a place of reconciliation where true unity exists?

Dinner. Breaking bread. Coming together around a table. There is something sacred and inviting about gathering around a meal. It provides an organic opportunity for vulnerability, honest conversations, and intimate relationship building. During the Last Supper they gathered around a meal, sitting with their brokenness, sinfulness, and differences, and found themselves in the presence of Jesus. That is what happens at At The Table.

During any At The Table Dinner Worship Experience, you will see the sanctuary filled with round tables with six people sitting together shoulder to shoulder, passing around a bowl of lemon artichoke orzo while brushing different skin tones. You will hear varying vernacular offering more lemonade to their neighbor. You will see a Taiwanese-American restaurant manager, a Black PhD student, and a Latina makeup artist wrestling with discussion questions that encourage honest personal storytelling and active listening. You will see a Honduran-American hand-in-hand with a Jamaican-American praying over each other. You will see a White woman from Alabama side by side with a Black man from California worshipping in Spanish. You will see love. You will see family.

You will find hope. Hope that young people, regardless of race, gender, language, culture, past, you name it, are seeking to come together to be the body of Christ. It brings hope that church can still be a place of community and unity where the Spirit is tangibly moving. At The Table is not necessarily a place where racial reconciliation is talked about, rather, it is lived out. We do not have to wait until heaven to be heaven. The beauty of joyful coexistence in heaven can be here now, as it should. On earth as it is in heaven.

# Reflection

What strikes you about Woo's story of At the Table? What actions could you take to make your community look like heaven now? What would healing racialization look like if this story took place in your congregation?

# Closing Vision

*After this I looked, and there was a great crowd that no one could number.*
*They were from every nation, tribe, people, and language.*
*They were standing before the throne and before the Lamb.*
*(Revelation 7:9 CEB)*

God gave me (Stephanie) a clear vision, and placed opportunities and people in my life to begin the journey. I am called to the journey of manifesting the vision we see in Revelation 7:9, through the conduit of The United Methodist Church. What John Wesley began, we are called by God to fulfill and perfect.

Charles Wesley penned to paper, in 1792, a Methodist hymn "A Charge to Keep I Have." During my ordination, the worship team sang this hymn, and the power of the Holy Spirit fell fully upon me. It was so thick that the only thing I could do was tell God, "Thank you," and worship God in my seat. I was struck by the second stanza, and even today when I hear it, it urges me to focus on "what's next?" What is God calling me to do next?

> *A charge to keep I have, a God to glorify,*
> *a never-dying soul to save, and fit it for the sky.*
>
> *To serve the present age, my calling to fulfill;*
> *O may it all my powers engage to do my Master's will!* [54]

Why? Because the earth is groaning. I do believe in this present age distinct African American, Latino American, African, Indian, Native American

---

54.   1 Wesley, Charles, "A Charge to Keep I Have," *The United Methodist Hymnal* (Nashville: The United Methodist Publishing House, 1989), 413, stanzas 1, 2.

faith communities are necessary because of the sinful nature of humanity. But there will be a day, and I believe it is happening now right before our eyes, that Revelation 7:9-15 will begin to manifest . . .

*After this I looked, and there was a great crowd that no one could number. They were from every nation, tribe, people, and language. They were standing before the throne and before the Lamb. They wore white robes and held palm branches in their hands. They cried out with a loud voice:*
> *"Victory belongs to our God*
> *who sits on the throne,*
> *and to the Lamb."*

*All the angels stood in a circle around the throne, and around the elders and the four living creatures. They fell facedown before the throne and worshipped God, saying,*
> *"Amen! Blessing and glory*
> *and wisdom and thanksgiving*
> *and honor and power and might*
> *be to our God forever and always. Amen."*

*Then one of the elders said to me, "Who are these people wearing white robes, and where did they come from?"*
*I said to him, "Sir, you know."*

*Then he said to me, "These people have come out of great hardship. They have washed their robes and made them white in the Lamb's blood. This is the reason they are before God's throne. They worship him day and night in his temple, and the one seated on the throne will shelter them.*

I believe this is the ultimate vision of our future. I also believe when we seek to heal racialization, we can pray with integrity the prayer of Jesus:

*"Pray, like this:*
> *Our Father who is in heaven,*
> *uphold the holiness of your name.*
> *Bring in your kingdom*
> *so that your will is done on earth as it's done in heaven."*
> *(Matthew 6:9-10)*

Christ points out that it is his will that we pray to seek. Not my will, the clergy's will, the people's will, nor the will of Satan, but the will of

God, in heaven and on earth; our submission to God's will is the game changer that leads to our salvation through the power of the Holy Spirit.

We can all be redeemed so that God may be glorified; therefore, we accept Christ as our head and love our neighbors, we receive the gift of eternal life and the foretaste of glory divine. When we live our lives through our faith in God, living into the will of our heavenly God, then our earthly presence includes worshipping with diverse groups of people.

The first Sunday of 2023, at one of the churches in which I live out my faith, I was looking out from the pulpit at the congregation. One of the visitors that day was a seminary student from Indonesia.

The lead pastor that morning had invited Hendra, the Indonesian seminary student, to come up to pray. He said prior to praying, "Hi, Family in Christ, I am Hendra from Indonesia, so let us pray to our Lord." Then he began to pray, in English and in the four other languages he spoke.

As Hendra prayed, God showed me a vision of multicultural, multi-ethnic churches being birthed. I had a vision during the prayer. I saw a man coming into the worship space in a wheelchair with no legs and parts of his hands missing. I saw in the back of the congregation, a twenty-something Anglo young adult, and on the other side of the congregation two more Anglo families. Tears began to fall down my face. This was his prayer:

> "Father you told the prophets and the apostles that one day every nation shall come to your table eating from the same table, because we are all your children. We are thankful Lord, because I am an Indonesian Christian that can be a part of this church, and the common table, where we can share life together with you, eat with you, and cry with you. We pray our eyes will be fixed to you, to your beauty. Our body will fade away, but our spiritual bodies will grow day by day. So that when we are face-to-face with you, we are strong in you, we are grateful you don't just live in the heights of the heavens, but we are grateful you are also here on earth, with us in our daily lives, where we live, walk, and eat with you. We ask your blessing of us, the family of St. Mark's, so that we may be a blessing for our city, so that we may join hand-in-hand with other churches in our communities. May we walk into this new year not with empty resolutions, but doing it from our heart,

so that what we do is what we say, and what we say is what we do. May your name be glorified by all nations. in your Son, Jesus's name we pray, Amen."

I opened my tear-filled eyes, and I said to our lead pastor sitting beside me, "Well, Doc, we just became an international church where every tongue, tribe, and nation will worship God, together." As I stood up to speak to the congregation, I looked out over the room and saw the man in his wheelchair with no legs and parts of his hands missing praising God. I saw a young Anglo adult woman praising God. And on the other side of the congregation, two Anglo families praising God, with African and African American brothers and sisters all worshipping God together.

I believe there is a time when a great crowd from every nation, tribe, people, and language will worship the Lamb of God, with loud voices crying out: "Victory belongs to our God who sits on the throne, on earth as it is in heaven."

We can do justice together. Now is the time.

# The Next Step

- Throughout the book we have referenced companion resources:

1. The Doing Justice Together audio/video stories at the Fresh Expressions channel on Amplify Media found here: https://my.amplifymedia.com/freshexpressions/home

2. The *Doing Justice Together: Background & Context* e-book is designed to support and document in depth many of the ideas that are assumed here. If your team is skeptical of racialization, or wants to go deeper with its origins, or wants a thorough biblical and theological treatment, start here. (Find the e-book at abingdonpress/doingjusticetogether.com.)

3. We suggest utilizing the ecosystem of resources as a team and perhaps inviting the entire congregation into a study, sermon series, or town hall gathering.

4. Finally, Stephanie and Michael are available to journey along-side you as you explore the healing racialization pathway. If you need coaching and/or training, you can reach out to them directly through their websites: https://www.stephaniehand. com/ or https://michaeladambeck.com/.

Printed in the USA
CPSIA information can be obtained
at www.ICGtesting.com
LVHW021307030124
767593LV00001B/4